Twayne's English Authors Series

Sylvia E. Bowman, *Editor*

INDIANA UNIVERSITY

Dorothy Richardson

TEAS 187

Dorothy Richardson

DOROTHY RICHARDSON

By THOMAS F. STALEY
University of Tulsa

TWAYNE PUBLISHERS
A DIVISION OF G. K. HALL & CO., BOSTON

Library of Congress Cataloging in Publication Data

Staley, Thomas F
    Dorothy Richardson.

    (Twayne's English authors series ; TEAS 187)
    Bibliography: p. 135-42.
    Includes index.
    1.   Richardson, Dorothy Miller, 1873-1957 — Criticism
and interpretation.   I.   Title.
PR 6035.I34Z93   823'.9'12   76-8009
ISBN 0-8057-6662-6

To J. Paschal Twyman
Builder of Libraries
and dear friend

Contents

About the Author

Thomas F. Staley is Professor of English and Dean of the Graduate School of the University of Tulsa, where he also edits the *James Joyce Quarterly*. He was a Fulbright professor in Trieste in 1966 and 1971, and a recipient of an American Council of Learned Societies Grant in 1969. He has written or edited five books on James Joyce, among them the commemorative volume: *Ulysses: Fifty Years* (1974), and with Bernard Benstock, *Approaches to Ulysses: Ten Essays* (1970). Staley has also written widely on modern literature; his essays have appeared in many journals, among them *Southern Review, Mosaic, Modern Fiction Studies, Commonweal, Studies in the Novel, Études Anglaises,* and the *Journal of Modern Literature*. He has lectured throughout Europe and the United States, chaired three of the International James Joyce Symposia, and served as President of the James Joyce Foundation from 1969 - 73.

Preface

In a recent article in the *Sewanee Review*, Charles T. Harrison observed with some scorn that "One of the conspicuous features of recent literary criticism is its addiction to 'approaching' people and things." This book is no exception, but it attempts in its investigation to be more than simply an approach to Dorothy Richardson and her work. In short, it attempts to examine not only the major aspects of her literary career but also the influence, the cultural background, and the literary merits and faults of the works themselves. My bias is, I hope, a clear one. I have not tried to make large claims for Miss Richardson's literary stature; on the other hand, I have tried to indicate with sufficient literary evidence just what her accomplishments were and, in so doing, to state as reasonably as possible her contribution to modern British literature. The final judgment is, of course, left to the reader.

The central core of Miss Richardson's work is *Pilgrimage*, the collective title of thirteen self-contained novels, which she referred to as "chapters." To each of these chapters she gave a title, and the majority were published separately; in this study, they are treated both separately and collectively. It is solely upon *Pilgrimage* that Miss Richardson's contribution to modern literature rests. Because most of her literary career was devoted to the writing of *Pilgrimage*, my study follows the development of this single work. Appropriately interspersed within my study are various sections which deal with literary influences, comparisons, and her minor works. It seemed that this organizational structure was the most effective way to treat Miss Richardson's literary development. The first chapter is devoted to a narrative of her life, and the remaining portions are an extended critical treatment of her work.

In this study I have avoided the singularity of approach that derives from propounding a particular thesis; in fact, I have found myself blunting certain critical arguments which I felt inappropriate to my major purpose of providing a coherent account of Dorothy Richardson's artistic development and a general point of view.

I should like to express my gratitude to the New York Public Library, especially to the curators of the Berg Collection who gave me access to Miss Richardson's letters to P. B. Wadsworth. To Mr. Wadsworth himself I owe a special debt for generous advice and for sharp counsel about the life and times of Dorothy Richardson. Professor Gloria Glikin's research on the life of Dorothy Richardson is acknowledged in the text, but I owe her a special debt for supplying me with the biographical data in Chapter 1. It is with pleasure that I acknowledge the research of Maggie Neville for her help with Chapter 1 and the help of Francis C. Bloodgood, formerly of the University of Tulsa, for his invaluable aid in the preparation of the manuscript.

I am deeply indebted to the University of Tulsa for awarding me a research grant during the course of this study, and to the Fulbright sponsors in both the United States and Italy, who on two occasions, five years apart, provided me with the opportunity to both begin and complete this work.

Page references for *Pilgrimage* have been inserted directly into the text in parentheses, the details of which are indicated in the footnote for the first citation.

I am grateful to Alfred A. Knopf in New York and J. M. Dent in London for permission to quote from *Pilgrimage*.

THOMAS F. STALEY

University of Tulsa

Chronology

1873   Dorothy Miller Richardson born May 17, in Abingdon, Berkshire, England, the third of four children.

1884 - Attends Southwest London College, a private school.
1890

1891   Leaves home to go as a pupil-teacher to a school in the ~ province of Hanover, Germany.

1891 - Teaches at Miss Ayre's school in Finsbury Park, North
1893   London.

1893 - Serves as governess to children of upper-class family in
1895   London's West End.

1896   Beginning of a long, intimate association with H. G. Wells.

1896 - Begins London career as a dental assistant.
1907

1902   First article appears in *The Outlook*, an obscure, anarchist monthly.

1905   Trip to Bernese Oberland, Switzerland.

1906   Trip to Vaud, Switzerland.

1906 - Writes reviews and essays for *Ye Crank* and *The Open*
1907   *Road*, unconventional monthlies.

1908 - Contributes descriptive sketches to *The Saturday Review*.
1914

1913   *Consumption Doomed* and *Some Popular Foodstuffs Exposed*, a translation.

1914   Translates *Man's Best Food*. Publishes *The Quakers Past and Present* and *Gleanings from the Works of George Fox*.

1915   Contributes eleven signed articles and writes anonymous monthly column for *The Dental Record*. Publishes *Pointed Roofs*, her first novel.

1916   *Backwater.*
1917   *Honeycomb.* Marries Alan Odle, an artist.
1919   *The Tunnel* and *Interim.*
1921   *Deadlock.*
1923   *Revolving Lights.*
1925   *The Trap.*
1927   *Oberland.*
1927 -   Contributes articles to *Close Up*, a magazine of the cinema.
1933
1930   *John Austen and the Inseparables*, a critical study.
1931   *Mammon*, a translation. Publishes *Dawn's Left Hand.*
1932   Translates *The DuBarry* and *André Gide: His Life and His Work.*
1934   *Jews in Germany*, a German translation; *Silent Hours*, a French translation.
1935   *Clear Horizon.*
1938   *Pilgrimage*, four volumes.
1944   Begins thirteenth part of *Pilgrimage (March Moonlight).*
1948   Death of Alan Odle.
1957   Death, June 17, at Beckenham in Kent.
1967   Reissue of Omnibus Edition of *Pilgrimage* including previously unpublished *March Moonlight.*

CHAPTER 1

The Woman — The Writer — The Work

I The Early Years

THE life of Dorothy Miller Richardson was, at least in its outward contours, uneventful, difficult, and shadowed by poverty during her adult years. Yet writer Winifred Bryher "told [her] friends abroad that if they want to know what England was like between 1890 and 1914, they must read *Pilgrimage*. . . ."[1] No single vision of life is, of course, complete, especially when it reflects the contemporary ambiance of the writer; but Miss Richardson's depiction of life in England during this period focuses more broadly on the cross sections of English life than, for example, does the work of George Gissing at one extreme and the writing of Virginia Woolf at the other. Gissing wrote of the desperately poor who were victims of the turmoil of social and economic forces during this period, and Virginia Woolf was a part of the Bloomsbury elite which represented a life far removed from the lower and the growing middle class in England. Since Dorothy Richardson's world lies between these two poles, Bryher's suggestion is in this sense an accurate one. Because *Pilgrimage* is highly autobiographical, it offers a broadly representative picture of English life at the close of the nineteenth century and at the beginning of the twentieth.

Pilgrimage, in both theme and content, is a work which reflects many of the issues and attitudes of the age in which it was written. Bryher regards Dorothy Richardson as a revolutionary who fought not for dogmas but for the elementary rights of women who, treated like slaves, were denied even the most elementary rights of education and of economic security.[2] Despite the revolutionary character that Bryher describes, Dorothy Richardson was a part of her times, too, in that she considered sex and money as typical Victorian taboos and was very slow in writing specifically about either subject. But

13

the struggle of young women, especially the underpaid and ex-
ploited group of working girls, is treated again and again in
Pilgrimage. The heroine's early socialist leanings and her animosity
toward men are deeply rooted in her rebellion against the severe
social codes and customs of Victorian England — and the life of
Miriam Henderson, the heroine of *Pilgrimage*, is the life experience
of her creator.

In order to appreciate more fully one of the most interesting, if not
most significant, literary accomplishments of twentieth-century
British fiction, it is helpful for the reader to separate first the
thirteen-part journey of the heroine into the components of the
author's own life. Miss Richardson is surely Miriam Henderson from
the first moments of *Pointed Roofs* (1915) to the last nuances of
March Moonlight (1938). Although *Pilgrimage* through *Dimple Hill*
(1938), the penultimate section, covers only a twenty-three-year seg-
ment in time from Miriam Henderson's seventeenth year until she
begins to write when near the age of forty, Dorothy Richardson's
literature was created from the experiences of her entire life.

Two strong forces struggled from the beginning to rule Dorothy
Richardson's life. Her paternal ancestors, the Richardsons, were
Puritans, a family of stern, restrained tradespeople. The Taylors, her
maternal forebears, were Anglican gentry of the West country who
engaged in manufacturing and in landholding.[3] To Dorothy, her
mother's people had jollity and cheerfulness (light) that fused with
the meditation and austerity of the Richardsons (dark). As she
described the effect, "It was immensely disturbing to be pressed
upon by two families, to discover in their different qualities, the ex-
planation of oneself" (I, 247).[4]

Thomas Richardson, Dorothy's paternal grandfather, was a grocer
in the southern county of Berkshire in Abingdon near Oxford. His
son Charles entered the family business as a young man.[5] On 18 July
1866, the worldly, angular, blond Charles Richardson married Mary
Miller Taylor, a fragile, dark, wild-spirited girl. To this union were
born four girls, Frances Kate, Alice Mary, Dorothy Miller, and
Jessie. The father, disappointed that Dorothy, his third child, had
not been a male heir, retained his wish by often referring to her as
his son.[6]

By the time Dorothy was born on 17 May 1873, her father Charles
Richardson had become a prosperous grocer and had raised his
family's position to the class of those living in Albert Park.[7] Wanting
to leave the trades, Charles took advantage of the opportunity when

his father died; he became a "gentleman" in 1874 by renting his
business and taking possession of an eight thousand pound in-
heritance.[8] The Richardsons were again to move upward in English
society, for Dorothy's father, who reveled in newly found avocations,
became an amateur patron of the arts and a spectator of science. He
soon joined the British Association for the Advancement of Science
and referred to himself as a member of the gentry.[9] Dorothy's early
years were lived in comparable luxury, and she once remarked that
she never knew until her adulthood that all people did not flourish as
did her family.[10]

When five years of age, Dorothy Richardson attended a private
school where her interests dwelt upon reading and little else. At this
time her curiosity and her sensitive awareness to "things" were
awakening. Interest in learned knowledge was substituted by a
fascination for objects that could be apprehended or encountered
directly[11]:

From the first I hated, and whenever possible evaded, orderly instruction.
. . . Not that I lacked the child's faculty of wonder. In a sense, I had it to ex-
cess. For what astonished, and still astonishes, me more than anything else
was the existence, anywhere, of anything at all. But since things there were,
I preferred to become one with them, in the child's way of direct apprehension which no subsequent "knowledge" can either rival or destroy, rather
than to stand back and be told, in regard to any of the objects of my self-
losing adoration, this and that. These objects were chiefly the garden, as
known to me when no one was about, the woods, the sky, and sunlight.[12]

After Mr. Richardson's introduction into the genteel class, he frequently took his family to Dawlish on the Sea; and this area introduced young Dorothy to the contrast of her two lifelong visions —
the sea and the garden[13]: "she reflected, remembering . . . the cliff
edge beyond Dawlish, the sun shining on pinkish sandy scrub, the
expression of the bushes; hurrying home with the big rough spaniel.
. . . She tried to remember when the strange independent joy had
begun, and thought she could trace it back to a morning in the garden at Babington . . ." (I, 316 - 17).

From 1881 to 1883 the Richardsons lived at Worthing on the
Channel Coast in Sussex. Dorothy resented the atmosphere of the
village school and disliked the church named St. Botolph because of
the unpleasant sound of the name,[14] and her sensitive awareness
reminds one of James Joyce's Stephen Dedalus who early associated

reality with words. In 1883, when Charles Richardson came into more money, possibly through speculation, he moved his family to Putney, a southwestern suburb of London[15]; and, for Dorothy, this home "became for me, from the moment we turned in . . . to pull up in front of the deep porch of a friendly-faced, many windowed house, a continuous enchantment."[16]

At Putney, the Richardson girls lived in luxury surrounded by sunken tennis courts, servants, good music, and education. Charles Richardson maintained the services of a governess for his daughters during their first years in London. Dorothy rebelled at this learning situation which exhibited the mode of education for girls of her day, "the minimum of knowledge and a smattering of various accomplishments."[17] When Dorothy Richardson was eleven, she and her younger sister Jessie were enrolled in Miss Harriet Sandell's private school for "daughters of gentlemen." In a new-found world of intellection, the curious Dorothy was introduced to John Ruskin and to Robert Browning. She also studied French and German, as well as mathematics, science, logic, and psychology. The last, "however, with its amazing claims, aroused from the first, uneasy skepticism."[18] At the school, she developed her interest in music, especially for the piano; for her talent was encouraged and promoted by home concerts in which the classics were featured. Dorothy's sensitivity to sound was important throughout her life, and it also manifests itself again and again in heroine Miriam's musical competence.[19] Until the age of seventeen, Dorothy Richardson was exposed to the culture and opportunities of the English upper middle class, but this style of life ended abruptly.

Charles Richardson was destined for financial failure. The years at Putney had absorbed the financial reserve from his father's business and his own speculations finally failed. By 1888, the signs of his declining fortune made themselves evident. In that same year, almost as a final burst of indulgence, he took a trip to America with the British Association. The next two years revealed the Richardson difficulties: servants were dismissed, and the girls were soon involved in finding outside employment.[20] After her seventeenth birthday in 1890, Dorothy applied for a teaching position in the German province of Hanover. Accepted as an English teacher and accompanied there by her father in early 1891, the fair-haired, fair-skinned, maturing Dorothy Richardson began her pilgrimage which started with the Saratoga trunk and the pointed roofs of Hanover.[21]

Dorothy's six months in this city are relived by Miriam Henderson in her experiences at Fraulein Pfaff's school for girls. Miriam's love of music is encouraged by the long hours spent in the *Saal* with the piano. Eventually, because of jealousy on the part of the Fraulein, the young, inexperienced teacher returned to England. Many of Miss Richardson's real observations as an instructor are reflected in the book appropriately entitled *Pointed Roofs* because of the architecture of Hanover. When she returned home in the middle of 1891, she was disillusioned; and she was "convinced that many of the evils besetting the world originated in the enclosed particularist home and in the institutions preparing women for such homes."[22] On her arrival in England, she found that her world was changing. Two of her sisters were soon to be married, but the third daughter had assumed the role of a governess. She realized that she, too, must seek employment; the Putney home of the Richardsons would never be the same again.[23]

From October 1891, to April 1893, Dorothy Richardson was employed as a teacher in the private school in Finsbury Park of the Misses Ayres who later become the fictional Misses Pyrnnes. Her stay there is recorded in the second novel of *Pilgrimage* called *Backwater* (1916). Miriam has returned to the past, the "backwater," not to a flowing stream but to a pool filled with memories and associations of her family from which she cannot flee. At the Misses Pyrnnes', Miriam comes in contact with a feminine atmosphere and has few companions of her own age.

In 1893, Charles Richardson went bankrupt; and the family moved from Putney to a smaller house in Cheswick. Miss Richardson soon left the Ayres' school to take a teaching position as governess in an upper-class home in London's West End.[24] For the short time spent there, she lived in quiet luxury. Miriam experiences the attitudes and opinions of the West End society in *Honeycomb*, a title suggesting Miriam's life of ease as governess-teacher. The title also implies the lack of depth in the domestic atmosphere that Miriam finds in the Corries and in their friends. In *Honeycomb* (1917), Dorothy Richardson also related by internal monologue the death of her mother who apparently had suicidal tendencies which needed attention long before she plunged a butcherknife into her throat. By the summer of 1895, Dorothy had assumed the responsibility of caring for her mother; and Mrs. Richardson's death concluded a seaside visit to Hastings in late autumn.[25] Dorothy Richardson, now twenty-two, had been away from home almost five years.

II *The Early London Years*

In 1896, Miss Richardson's life took a new direction that became a determining factor for the rest of her life: she took a job in the business world. Her move into the realms of masculine dominion reflected her growing view toward emancipation and woman's role in the late Victorian era.[26] Dorothy Richardson began her London career "never giving a thought to all [she] had left behind. In its place stood London and what London can mean as a companion."[27] Her job was that of a dental assistant and secretary in a successful West End dental office. Her employer, Harry Badcock, later a well-known figure in dentistry, was often mentioned in the pages of *The Dental Record* to which Miss Richardson later contributed.[28] The fictional prototype dentist is Mr. Hancock for whom Miriam works in *The Tunnel* (1919), the fourth novel in *Pilgrimage*. Suggesting the process of "maturation" and development, the title of the novel based on this experience blends the womb, the "dark journey," and the struggle into self-awareness, one which is finally accomplished by the lonely walk through the "tunnel."

When Miss Richardson took the position in London, she established residence in a Bloomsbury attic room on Endsleigh Street (Tansley Street) and became acquainted with the various aspects of London life. She recorded her feelings in "Data for Spanish Publisher": "I found all these islands to be the habitation of fascinating secret societies to each of which in turn I wished to belong and yet was held back, returning to solitude and to nowhere, where alone I could be everywhere at once, hearing all the voices in chorus."[29] The voices "in chorus" that Dorothy Richardson would hear in her years in London included writers, religious groups (Roman Catholic, Unitarian, and Quaker), political collections (Conservative Primrose League, Independent Labor Party, and Russian anarchists) and scientific and philosophic lectures.[30]

She attended the speeches of Basil Wilberforce, Rector of St. John's and Canon of Westminister, and heard lectures by Ellis McTaggart of Trinity College. She was searching for spiritual meaning in her life at this point, for Miss Richardson had already closed her mind to Christianity — at least in part. She rebelled against the masculine image of God as was posed by the clerics: "For their God demanded, first and foremost docility, fear, blind obedience, and a constant need of praise and adulation . . . all typically masculine demands."[31] During this early period of her new life in London she met many of the people with whom she would have lifelong associations. Charles Daniel, a free thinker, became her close friend. She roved the city avenues with Benjamin Grad, a young Russian Jew, newly arrived in England. Grad bore a striking resemblance to Michael Shatov, Miriam's first love interest in *Pilgrimage*, who appears first in *The Tunnel* and reappears in other novels. A reference perhaps to Benjamin Grad was mentioned in a letter to an acquaintance from Miss Richardson who was remembering an evening spent in the heart of London with friends. She related that "the dear thing [Benjamin Grad] can be very charming, attracts most women quite deeply for a while, but everyone who has taken him over has eventually bowed out. . . . Poor [name marked out] has always been one of our problems. The assimilated Jew is usually an unhappy creature."[32] The ancient Hebrew heritage of Michael Shatov is the source for much of Miriam's conflict through *Pilgrimage*.

The first years of Dorothy Richardson's introduction to London led her into a new world. People, places, and ideas took on a new significance of importance. She could act in relation to "things." The archipelago offered challenge — and also perhaps an ultimate purpose for her life. However, she often felt confused and bewildered as if still continuing in a "tunnel"; although it was bright at both ends far away, the light from the extremities did not permeate the present dimness: "Now and again all seemed darkness within and without, but always I failed to achieve try as I would, a complete despair."[33] The manifested experiences of the London life were part of her "becoming," but her true sense of reality and identity was elusive until she could acknowledge the "being" within her, reconciled to the "becoming," for a consequent real vision of life.[34]

With the meeting of new friends, Dorothy Richardson found herself renewing a girlhood association, one that affected her entire life. Amy Catherine Robbins, a companion from the Putney years, had become the wife of a promising writer, H. G. Wells.[35] In *The Tunnel* Dorothy recorded this reminiscence: "On the table lay a letter . . . from Alma [Amy]. . . . Of course Alma had answered the post card . . . it had been an impulse, a cry of triumph after years of groping about . . ."(II, 77). When Amy and her husband, who lived in Heatherlea, Worchester Park, Surrey, invited the young dental assistant to visit them there, her first acceptance of their first invitation led to others. Wells introduced Miss Richardson to a world of literature and scientific socialism which she had never known. In 1896, at thirty, he had already published *The Time Machine*, *The Wonderful Visit*, and a number of short stories.[36] The times spent both in Surrey and in Kent with Amy and her husband provided a background of material for Miss Richardson's intimate portrait of Wells in a later portion of *Pilgrimage*.

The fifth "chapter" of *Pilgrimage*, called *Interim* (1919), reveals the standstill that occurred for Dorothy Richardson before her first decade in London was completed. She had become dissatisfied with her job as secretary and was trying to synthesize her experiences into a knowledge of herself. In her journey for understanding and purpose, this was a waiting period. One certainty did emerge — she wanted to write; and, by 1903, Miss Richardson had begun to contribute articles for publication. Her contact with H. G. Wells had caused her to view the present society through the eyes of an anarchist; consequently, she wrote for magazines which oracled her new opinions. Her first article, unsigned, was printed in *The Outlook*, in October 1902.[37]

In another place she recorded: "I had begun to write. Translations and free-lance journalism had promised release from routine work that could not engage the essential forces of my being. The small writing table in my attic became the centre of my life."[38] While still living in the Endsleigh Street boardinghouse, her thoughts for possibly her most structurally perfect novel were formed: the sixth "chapter," *Deadlock*, was the result. As the title implies, she had reached a position in which it was impossible to proceed into a writing career. Her job had become increasingly routine, and she had fallen in love for the first time. "Experiments in being engaged to be married were not entirely satisfactory . . . on more than one occasion I withdrew a provisional pledge."[39]

In *Revolving Lights* (1923), the seventh "chapter," Miriam has frequent encounters with revolutionaries whose causes offer her sudden coruscations. Ideas and theories of reform vie for her loyalties. The lights of each, offering solace and solution to internal conflicts, "revolve" continually; for they never give her complete truth and lucidity. "The truth hidden below the surfaces of life was to yield itself to her slowly, imperceptibly, unpleasurably" (III, 396). Miriam's experiences in *Revolving Lights* reveal a period of Dorothy Richardson's life in which she sought new directions: she had been in London almost ten years.

In 1905, Miss Richardson moved from the Endsleigh Street home to a room in Woburn Walk. This narrow passage led to Flaxman Terrace and was nearly under the shadow of St. Pancras Church in Upper Woburn Place.[40] She recorded in *The Trap* (1925), her eighth "chapter," a description of her heroine's new surroundings: "A short by-street paved from side to side. Narrow housefronts and the end-most houses, hiding the passage that curved round into the further street, high enough to keep out of sight the neighbouring cubes of model dwellings and to leave, as principal feature in the upper air, the tower of St. Pancras Church. An old little street. A scrap of old London standing apart, between the Bloomsbury squares and the maze of streets toward the city" (III, 399). This passage gives the reader an impression of tightly wrought prose suggesting a closure or a "trap," and Miriam has reached a point of physical and emotional desperation. During her time spent at Flaxman's Court, Miriam sees and becomes familiar with W. B. Yeats who lives across the street and who had patronized the same dentist for whom she had worked in London.[41]

Because of general fatigue, Dorothy Richardson was encouraged to take a trip away from London. Dr. Badcock offered to pay for the excursion, and she thus made a visit to Oberland in Switzerland where she recuperated. This trip provided her with material for her ninth "chapter," appropriately named *Oberland* (1927).[42] The renewing experiences on the Swiss Alps restored her strength, but she returned to London and Harley Street still dissatisfied with her job.

Miss Richardson revealed to the reader her growing, intimate relationship with H. G. Wells in the tenth "chapter" of *Pilgrimage*, *Dawn's Left Hand* (1931) — a title which achieves significance in several ways. The "dawn," the first light before sunrise, indicates another possible pseudolight for Miriam to follow before the actual illumination. The term "left hand" implies a placing of oneself on the left side of a situation, such as to marry morganatically and to receive no share in possessions or dignities beyond the "morning gift." Hence, in *Dawn's Left Hand*, Miriam, who seeks another solution or "light" through love, knows that the affair is ironically a "darkness before dawn." Because the two worlds of Miriam Henderson and Hypo G. Wilson are far apart, she can receive only the morning gift, the left hand of dawn.

It is difficult to know when the association of Wells and Miss Richardson became a serious one. Their meeting in 1906 had begun a friendship strengthened by her visits to his home in Kent and the Wells' holidays in London which always included her. The portrait drawn of Wells as Hypo G. Wilson, which begins in *The Tunnel* and which Miss Richardson identified as that of Wells, is startling and determined. Since the portrayal reflects nuances of expression and her ambiguous attitudes toward the relationship, the reasons for, or the effects of, the relationship between Wells and the fledgling writer are difficult to determine. In an article concerning these years, Vincent Brome published valuable information resulting from conversations with Dorothy Richardson about Wells. During the interview she picked up an edition of *Pilgrimage* and began to read a section of *Revolving Lights* which showed a cheerful, affectionate Wilson at his home in Kent where he and Alma were visited by Miriam. Miss Richardson began to read aloud and then stopped short, saying "My novel was distinctly autobiographical. Hypo was Wells, Miriam in part myself and Alma Mrs. Wells."[43]

Then she selected a more intimate section from *Dawn's Left Hand* about a hotel-room rendezvous between Miriam and Hypo: "she found his arms about her in their turn and herself, surprised and not able with sufficient swiftness to contract her expanded being that still seemed to encompass him, rocked unsatisfactorily to and fro while his voice, low and shy and with the inappropriate unwelcome charm in it of the ineffectual gestures of a child learning a game, echoed the unsuitable words" (IV, 232). Miss Richardson laid the book aside and remarked directly to Brome: "I think that catches him as a lover . . . never completely lost . . . marred in the end by self-consciousness."[44] To her interviewer she made one last statement concerning the man who had so deeply marked her life. "He was rather ugly without his clothes."[45]

Because of the fictional account, the critical question arises as to whether or not the readers of *Pilgrimage* are prepared for the affair of Miriam Henderson and Hypo G. Wilson. Miriam, true to her creator, is most reluctant to discuss either money or sex throughout the entire journey of *Pilgrimage*. Her experience of falling in love with Michael Shatov is handled adroitly but in a typical Victorian manner. Miriam often seems to be so sexless and so prudish that she would not appear capable of commanding the situation that occurs in *Dawn's Left Hand*. One can only speculate as to why Miss Richardson became so personally involved with H. G. Wells. She admired Wells' intelligence but not all of his ideas; he had regard for her talent and encouraged her to write; and her maternal instinct and need for enlightenment, combined with Wells' brilliance and charm, could have stimulated the serious bond. His friendship, perhaps, gave her a needed source of "reality" which could have fostered the deep tie between them. He had given Miss Richardson financial help. But, in spite of this close relationship, his literary influence on her was limited. Nevertheless, Wells and Miss Richardson kept in contact during the rest of his life; and, when he became ill in 1944, she was invited by friends to stay near his home; but could not because of her own failing health. When Wells died in 1946, the news of his death "drove very deep."[46]

III   *New Decisions: Journalism and Fiction*

In 1906, Dorothy Richardson not only took a second trip to Switzerland, this time to Vaud, but also made some new decisions. As the title of the eleventh "chapter" of *Pilgrimage, Clear Horizon,* (1935), indicates, she now had little family to be concerned with, her father having gone to live with her sister Kate. Since her socio-political and Christian involvements in London were finished, nothing was left to bind her. In a critical analysis of *Pilgrimage,* Caesar Blake remarked of Miriam that "the same final repudiation of orthodox Christianity and socialism leaves her equally free for the future. . . . She had once said of herself that she always left things to be decided or acted upon the horizon. *The horizon is clear.*"[47] Miss Richardson gave Dr. Badcock notice and left the world of dentistry to become a journalist. She wrote of her venture in a letter to Joseph Prescott: "Sixty years ago, . . . a palmist asked whether I had done any writing . . . my reply in the negative, brought from her just two words: Begin now. . . ."[48]

During the years of 1906 and 1907, after leaving the Harley Street dentist's office, Dorothy Richardson wrote for several unorthodox magazines, *Ye Crank* and *The Open Road,* both edited by her freethinking friend Charles Daniel. Her articles ranged from "Days with Walt Whitman" (a review) to "Thearchy and Socialism" (an essay).[49] When she escaped to the country in 1907 to write, she spent some time at a Quaker fruit farm on Windmill Hill on the coast of Sussex; and this experience was personally gratifying. She had moved in her thinking from anarchism and communism to socialism, denying communism for its lack of attention to the individual. The Quaker philosophy introduced her to mysticism and to the quest for a reality that bypassed ordinary perception in order to establish a unity with the Absolute through supersensuous, non-rational processes.[50] For the Quakers, the experience of mysticism "is not a gift of grace to a few, but possible to every man by virtue of his partaking of the spirit of God in himself."[51] This association with the Friends finally seemed to bring forth an answer to an existent reality within herself, a mystic way on which she journeyed continually. The mystic thought which would later influence many of Miss Richardson's works was made manifest in *Dimple Hill*, her twelfth "chapter" of *Pilgrimage*, which is set in the heart of a Quaker community.

While at Windmill Hill, Miss Richardson began to contribute regularly to *The Saturday Review*, an activity which lasted for six years until 1913.[52] Gloria Glikin has remarked about the importance of the sketches that Dorothy Richardson wrote in those six years to her thirteen-part work: "they foreshadow *Pilgrimage* in the methods she chose for presenting her material. She wished to convey a sense of immediacy, in order to implicate the reader, and she wanted to be the agent of transmission. . . . *The Saturday Review* sketches reveal Dorothy Richardson writing from the beginning out of what she knows, as the person who knows, at the moment of knowing. She was writing, essentially, in the autobiographical manner."[53]

During this time, Miss Richardson left the coast of Sussex and Windmill Hill and moved upcountry to a scene near Hailsham and Hurstmonceaux. Because her only income came from the *Saturday Review* sketches, and because she wished to supplement her financial reserve, she decided to write a column for *The Dental Record;* and she did so for the years 1915 to 1919.[54] The opportunity for expression urged her on, and she used for her writings in the professional magazine many of her opinions of social and political problems currently important. Miss Richardson's lay knowledge of the dental profession also enabled her to contribute valuable articles concerning new methods and techniques in the field.[55]

IV   *Beginning the Novel*

The years since she had left the Harley Street dentist's office had not been easy ones. During her time away from London, several friends offered her residence and assistance. In the year before *Pilgrimage* was begun, Miss Richardson lived with new friends, Mr. and Mrs. J. D. Beresford in the village of St. Ives on the tip of the Southwestern coast.[56] In 1913, she was lent a cottage in Cornwall which had been converted from a chapel into a study.[57] With solitude and ten shillings a week, she began to write the novel about her own life. Bryher, a friend of the author in later years, related the hardships which Miss Richardson endured in the months of writing the first "chapter" of the novel: "The purchase power of ten shillings then was equivalent, perhaps, to three pounds today but it had to cover fuel, light, food, and as she particularly insisted, paper.

She went without meals for two days to save the half crown that was necessary to post the manuscript to a publisher."[58] Dorothy Richardson, remembering the months at St. Ives, later remarked to Bryher: "I often think of it now when writers complain to me about lack of security and time."[59]

The resultant effort produced a manuscript in tiny, medieval handwriting, the first "chapter," *Pointed Roofs* — that made known a story which actually had begun to exist forty years before. Miss Richardson wrote of her decision to structure her work according to experience in "Data for Spanish Publisher":

The material that moved me to write would not fit the framework of any novel I had experienced. I believed myself to be, even when most enchanted, intolerant of the romantic and the realist novel alike. Each, so it seemed to me, left out certain essentials and dramatized life misleadingly. Horizontally. Assembling their characters, the novelists developed situations, devised events, climax and conclusion. I could not accept their finalities. Always, for charm or repulsion, for good or ill, one was aware of the author and applauding, or deploring his manipulations. This, when the drama was a conducted tour with the author deliberately present telling his tale. Still more so when he imagined, as did Flaubert, that in confining himself to "Constatation" he remained imperceptible. In either case, what one was assured were the essentials seemed to me secondary to something I could not then define, and the curtain-dropping finalities entirely false to experience.[60]

Miss Richardson wanted to "produce a feminine equivalent of the current masculine realism."[61] She desired to show through the life of one woman the feminine consciousness — the pure being exposed to and surrounded by the surface reality. Miss Richardson felt that her novel must embody the flow of "being" which was caught up by torrents of the past, present, and future, disregarding time horizontally and elevating awareness to a transcendent plane. Again in "Data," Miss Richardson related that she was "aware, as she wrote, of the gradual falling away of the preoccupations that for a while had dictated the briskly moving script, and of the substitution, for these inspiring preoccupations, of a stranger in the form of contemplated reality having for the first time in her experience its own say."[62] Her character was to be Miriam Henderson, a seventeen-year-old Dorothy Richardson; and the pilgrimage was Miriam's alone. "How could anyone else describe her? No one else was there to describe her."[63]

Borrowing from Henry James, Miss Richardson created the

journey's narrative in the form of an inner and outer point of view of one person; and every experience is solely Miriam's, by and through herself. Caesar Blake has suggested the extent to which Miss Richardson used James' techniques:

Miss Richardson assimilated James's point-of-view, principle and something of his style, but she went beyond James's restriction to subtle analysis of subtle human problems. *Pilgrimage* ranges far more widely — and on purpose, more loosely — than James's novels did, and it pioneers a greater psychological depth within characterization by exploring levels of consciousness omitted in James's preoccupation with conscious intelligence. Miss Richardson, like James, immerses the reader in a sensibility but, unlike James, she is content to exploit the quality of that sensibility for its own sake.[64]

The influence of other authors upon her work is not extensive. She had not read Marcel Proust before she began *Pilgrimage* in 1913,[65] although she may have read both Virginia Woolf and James Joyce at a later date. At the age of forty, Dorothy Richardson had begun to relive her life through Miriam Henderson.

Pointed Roofs was rejected, and Miss Richardson returned to her periodical contributions. By this time, her fluency in French and German brought with it a new interest in the field of translating. In 1913, she rendered into English the French works *Consumption Doomed* and *Some Popular Foodstuffs Exposed* by Dr. Paul Carton. A German writer, Professor Gustave Kruger, authored *Man's Best Food*, which was translated by Miss Richardson in 1914. From her experiences with the Quakers, she wrote two books, *The Quakers Past and Present* and *Gleanings from the Works of George Fox*, both completed in 1914.[66] In September 1915, the manuscript of *Pointed Roofs* was published by Gerald Duckworth and labeled as "feminine impressionism."[67] Early 1916 found Dorothy Richardson again living in London and completing the second "chapter," *Backwater;* it was published by Duckworth who issued ten of the eventual thirteen parts of *Pilgrimage*.

V *Middle Years: Marriage*

She settled in St. John's Wood in a lodging inhabited by Bohemian writers and artists. From a new group of acquaintances appeared Alan Odle, an obscure painter who lived at the same boardinghouse. In 1916, the thin, pale Odle was twenty-eight and was supported financially by his father.[68] She may have been mater-

nally drawn toward him, and she may have also admired his reserved
intelligence and restraint. Glikin has written that "they shared . . .
an equal dislike of women."[69] Both lonely wanderers in a large city,
they were set apart from others by worlds of thought. Alan Odle
reflected his dark attitude in his portraits, and Miss Richardson
would reveal hers in *Pilgrimage*. At forty-four, she had taken as a
close confidant and as a companion a young artist doomed to
obscurity and tinsel fame; but she said that he had introduced her
into a new world, a missing link in her chain of being.[70] Against
protests, Alan Odle and Dorothy Richardson were married on 29
August 1917, when a threat of death hovered over him since he had
been diagnosed as a tubercular with a few months to live.[71] This
man, so different an embodiment of the masculinity which she
fought and admired ambivalently, was the third and final person of
the triune of men who strongly affected her life — Charles Richardson, H. G. Wells, and Alan Odle;[72] and her marriage with him was a
happy one.

As husband and wife, the Odles established residence in Cornwall
and soon started upon a yearly ritual which always began at their
three-season home near the sea and which was completed with
summer in London in Alan's rooms at St. John's Wood.[73] The city,
the beloved "companion," was Miss Richardson's again in a season
of utter awareness: "Summer is Eternity showing. . . . Summer is the
soul of man" (II, 403). For the next twenty-one years the Odles
divided their time between the two locales that were so much a part
of her work and her life — the sea (Cornwall) and the garden (London).

Dorothy Richardson became a wife with concentrated efforts at
domesticity. The role of the emancipated woman as the guardian of
the home became important. She cooked and cleaned as avidly as
she had composed *Pointed Roofs*. As hostess in their homes, she
commanded the tea table with as much efficiency and skill as she
had handled the delicate dental instruments on Harley Street.[74] The
shacks and cottages at Cornwall and the two rooms in St. John's
Wood were havens for her. Once more after a long estrangement,
the home became a vital source of happiness. When Bryher visited
the Odles in London some years after their marriage, she remarked
upon the scene and the surrounding atmosphere:

It was a narrow, drowsy, still almost Victorian street. . . . Miriam (and she
was Miriam) was just as I had expected to find her, with a stiff blouse and a

mass of gold hair piled on the top of her head. . . . A big table, sinking under the weight of Alan's books and drawings, almost filled the room (I was told later that it had once cracked in two), and he sat behind it, smoking and smiling, always ready to rescue Dorothy or turn the conversation if it bothered her, and otherwise watching visitors or the way the light fell on a door, with his brown, draughtsman's eyes. A fireplace almost filled the wall behind Dorothy's chair. They had pinned a row of post cards along its top, mostly of gargoyles from Notre Dame, and faded as these had become through smoke and fog, they were so essential a part of the decoration that I have never forgotten them.[75]

Four more of Dorothy Richrdson's chapters of *Pilgrimage* were completed and published within the first ten years of her marriage: *Honeycomb* (1917); *The Tunnel* (1919); *Interim* (1919); and *Deadlock* (1921). Also during their yearly cycle of moving, she managed to contribute more essays, stories, and reviews. As more of her books were printed, she began to be recognized in literary circles. Young women fighting for their elementary rights and reacting with fury against the traditional social conventions considered Dorothy Richardson to be their voice. For them, her art was the "flower of . . . deeply felt rebellion"[76]; and such youthful admirers often sought Miss Richardson in London during the summer months. She was "linked" by critics with Joyce and Proust and she may have met both Proust and Joyce through their books which were given to her and called to her attention in the 1920s by P. Beaumont Wadsworth, a prominent English journalist.[77] Miss Richardson could see that the fame and attainment of these writers and of others like Virginia Woolf were far outshadowing her meager success. However, she would do nothing for public favor; for, as she once remarked to Wadsworth in an interview, "I should love to be popular, but I would not lift a little finger to get it."[78] She even refused to be photographed.

When the 1920s brought financial difficulty for the Odles, Dorothy Richardson attempted to borrow money from friends.[79] She was not receiving royalties, and her husband was never able to contribute much to the upkeep of their existence. Aside from exhibiting occasionally and reproducing several black and whites for the American publication *Vanity Fair*, he was unable to contribute to their support.[80] Amid financial hardship, Dorothy Richardson recorded their yearly journey:

from our London flat, for which each winter a tenant had to be found, to Cornwall, for my husband's health, where in pre-war times retreats that in summer were worth many guineas per week, were gladly let for the winter months, for a song, to tenants who would keep the place dry and keep down the rats, and thence, from our winter solitude, for our annual spring holiday, to Trevone, hub of the Universe, with a shop, a post-office, and finally an omnibus: . . . thence our third move, the return to London and a few months of delightful social life plus visits to friends and relatives at a distance, until the equally delightful retreat, in the autumn to solitude.[81]

    Dorothy Richardson's middle years brought many friendships; most of these began in London during the summer season. She became acquainted with Ford Maddox Hueffer (Ford) and D. H. Lawrence.[82] When Lawrence was getting the publication of *Lady Chatterly's Lover* prepared in Florence, Miss Richardson sent brochures asking for subscriptions to the first edition.[83] In 1923 and 1924, when the Odles went to Paris for brief excursions, she met Ernest Hemingway and others in the group of Left Bank writers.[84] While the time at Cornwall was spent in relatively secluded activities, the Odles were quite busy with friends in London during the short summer months there.

    From 1927 to 1933, Dorothy Richardson contributed articles to *Close Up*, a publication started with the innovation of the motion picture and edited by Winifred Bryher and by her husband Kenneth McPherson; and Miss Richardson's interest in cinematic techniques is evidenced in her pictorial use of imagery.[85] In the 1930s, the Odle's financial difficulties were somewhat alleviated by an unexpected windfall: Miss Richardson was notified that she was to be the recipient of a trust fund established for artists who were temporarily in need. Established by Bryher, this beneficent gift helped the couple during a time of distress.[86] But the aid was not enough to support them during the lean 1930s. She began more translations, this time under burden and strain, of French and German works: *The Du Barry* by Karl Von Schumacher (German); *Jews in Germany* by Joseph Kastein (German); *André Gide: His Life and his Work* by Léon Pierre-Quint (French); *Silent Hours* by Robert de Traz (French); and *Die Macht*, a novel by Robert Neumann (German). She also wrote *John Austen and the Inseparables* during this period. The only apparent gain from this arduous task of translating was a name in the field, and her achievement did not affect her decision never to translate again.[87]

    In 1938, J. M. Dent and the Cresset Press published an omnibus edition of *Pilgrimage*, for the "chapters" were brought together to assure more readers a continuity from one part to another. Alfred

Knopf in the United States issued the publication on 28 November 1938.[88] In 1967 the omnibus edition was reissued by Knopf in New York and by J. M. Dent in London. This edition included an introduction by Walter Allen and the thirteenth volume, *March Moonlight*. Miss Richardson had agreed to the one edition although she knew that the twelfth chapter, *Dimple Hill*, did not complete *Pilgrimage*. She decided, however, that a posthumous issuance of the thirteenth chapter and of others to follow would be the only way of continuing the publishing of her life work. The sales from the 1938 Dent edition were small; only 699 volumes had been sold after the first three months of publication.[89]

VI *Later Years: Cornwall*

World War II came to change the fairly rhythmical life of the Odles. Their home in the winter at Cornwall had to be forsaken in exchange for a new residence called "Zansizzey," which was by the village of Padstow near Trevone.[90] Miss Richardson, during this latter part of her life, was granted a Civil List pension of one hundred pounds.[91] H. G. Wells had tried earlier to bring about such security for her but had failed.[92] For five years she entered into the times of war and hardship. Her domestic talents and clerical ability enabled her to help in an area besieged with war victims.[93] In 1944, the Odles settled in a new home, the last, called "Hillside," which was closer to the village and to the sea. They kept the interior decoration of their ground-floor villa as close to that of the London home as possible.[94] After a long lapse, Miss Richardson turned again to *Pilgrimage*. In her seventies, she seemed to receive a new vitality, a new faculty for her creative imagination: ". . . Dorothy Richardson believed that she was coming into possession of something always sought: a sense of time as vertical rather than horizontal. Events arranged themselves in a pattern of importance, not chronology — the kind of pattern, she said, that fiction at its best could offer."[95] Her three short stories — "Excursion," "Visitor," and "Visit" — were written as manifestations of this theory.[96]

Her friend H. G. Wells died in 1946. Wells and Alan Odle were the polar extremes of her life, but Wells' death added to her worry that she might die before her husband and leave him alone to care for himself. A sudden refutation came one morning at Hillside in February 1948, when Alan Odle died unexpectedly while walking to the village library. He was sixty; his wife had reached seventy-five; and they had been inseparable companions for thirty-one years.[97] As might be expected, Dorothy Richardson began after her husband's death a rapid decline in health and spirit. The home that had served as a scene for love, kindness, and laughter was changed. She withdrew into the depths of her own mind which had been the provision of another creation for so long. Revival came only at times, for it seemed more natural that Miss Richardson be living in her own private, psychic world. She suffered mental delusions. On occasion she would assume a blankness as "if special insights were at work."[98] It was as if the only verity of her life, the "pure being" deep within her, was transcending and overcoming the reality of the world to which she had paid only partial allegiance.

Miss Richardson remained at Hillside in Cornwall and continued to write letters, essays, short stories, and *Pilgrimage.* London newspapers welcomed her weekly journalism, which usually consisted of articles written on the role of the twentieth-century woman.[99] She took frequent walks to the village for tea; and she kept composing at her wooden table in large, scrawling lines, a handwriting that reflected her urgency and determination. She felt that the thirteenth "chapter" must be completed, that Miriam's journey would soon be ending. The cycle was accomplished: *Pointed Roofs* had begun with the ". . . *March* twilight that lay upon the landings . . . the staircase . . . almost dark" (I, 15). *Dimple Hill* had hinted of termination: "none of the summer days, no going forth to discover and explore, had brought so deep a pang of love as this sudden finding . . . of *autumn's* first breath . . . greeting her now . . ." (IV, 550). Spring came again with *March Moonlight,* left unfinished, another beginning.

In 1954 her nephew and sister-in-law, Rose Odle, moved Miss Richardson from the Cornwall home. She could no longer be alone, she needed care and attention, and her residence was to be a nursing home in Kent at Beckingham.[100] Later, visitors who came to see her remarked that the home was dreary and that she had none of her personal effects there, not even a picture[101]; but she did have a large, sunny room and could look into a garden.[102] On 17 June 1957, at the edge of summer, the first memory, the garden of childhood, became the last. Dorothy Richardson was surrounded by the "secret" she had always known since the "beginning of things," a mystic encounter with transcendency, a wellspring of being found "far away in the distance, coming always nearer, . . . the *summer morning* of her infancy, a permanent standing arrested, level with the brilliance of flower-heads . . . no movement but the hovering of bees. *Beyond* this memory towards which she passed every day more surely, a *marvelous scene unfolded* . . ." (III, 197).

CHAPTER 2

Pilgrimage — *The Journey Begins*

I   *The Search for Form*

IN 1938, the occasion of the publication of the "scattered
chapters" into the one four-volume collection *Pilgrimage*,
Dorothy Richardson wrote in the foreword:

> The lonely track, meanwhile, had turned out to be a populous highway.
> Amongst those who had simultaneously entered it, two figures stood out.
> One a woman mounted upon a magnificently caparisoned charger, the other
> a man walking, with eyes devoutly closed, weaving as he went a rich gar-
> ment of new words wherewith to clothe the antique dark material of his
> engrossment.
>
> News came from France of one Marcel Proust, said to be producing an un-
> precedentedly profound and opulent reconstruction of experience focused
> from within the mind of a single individual, and, since Proust's first volume
> had been published and several others written by 1913, the France of Balzac
> now appeared to have produced the earliest adventurer.
>
> Finally, however, the role of pathfinder was declared to have been played
> by a venerable gentleman, a charmed and charming high priest of nearly all
> the orthodoxies, inhabiting a softly lit enclosure he mistook, until 1914, for
> the universe, and celebrated by evolving, for the accommodation of his vast
> tracts of urbane commentary, a prose style demanding, upon the first
> reading, a perfection of sustained concentration akin to that which brought
> it forth, and bestowing, again upon the first reading, the recreative delights
> peculiar to this form of spiritual exercise. (I, 10 - 11)

The "lonely track" of revolution in prose fiction became peopled by
Virginia Woolf, James Joyce, Marcel Proust, and Henry James. In
this foreword, however, Miss Richardson, while aware that her contribution to the modern novel had been dimmed by these four major
writers, still sees her own artistic ambitions as lying in the same

sphere. In retrospect, she looks upon her work as having contributed in its particular way to the evolution of modern fiction. Her contribution was, of course, not on the scale of any of these four; but she has made a unique contribution in the development of the modern novel. As a result, the major purpose of this study is to evaluate the nature of this contribution by examining both the literary background and the *Pilgrimage* itself.

Those who have written literary histories of the "modern movement" in twentieth-century British prose fiction tend to assess Miss Richardson's work, even in passing, most closely with that of Virginia Woolf and James Joyce. This assumption is not completely accurate, for her writing is more nearly reflective of that of Henry James. *Pilgrimage* is also closer in its author's literary assumptions concerning the novel to the fictional theories of James rather than to those of Joyce or Virginia Woolf. Because of similarities in technique, Miss Richardson is linked with the latter two — and not without good reason. The preoccupation of earlier critics with comparisons of technique — especially one related to the stream-of-consciousness — tends, however, to detract from a more basic affinity which Miss Richardson has with James; and, in so doing, these critics have failed to realize what was really innovative in her work.

It was Henry James in his essay "The Art of Fiction" who raised the rhetorical questions which tended to blur the distinctions between the characters and the outward events to which the character in a work of fiction reacted. In this essay he asked: "What is character but the determination of incident? What is incident but the illustration of character?" On the other hand, James insisted that the novel's center is "the point of focus of all the rest." It is in Miriam Henderson, the heroine of *Pilgrimage*, that the entire work has its center and that the work, in James' words, finds "a principle of composition and contrives to hang together." In *Pilgrimage*, the inner world of the character is paramount; the outer world which Miriam experiences is only important in the way it contributes to the awareness of the self. This attitude toward character represents a radical departure from the fiction of John Galsworthy, Arnold Bennett, Wells, and earlier British novelists.

Alan Friedman in *The Turn of the Novel* explores the relationship between the formal organization of experience in fiction and the ethical assumptions that guide the form. He contends that the traditional premise about the design of experience in the eighteenth- and nineteenth-century novel was the premise of a closed experience. That is to say, the earlier novel rendered an expanding moral and emotional disturbance which promised all along to arrive at an ending that could and would check that foregoing expansion. But, Friedman[1] points out, in the twentieth century a new assumption about the nature and the end of experience slowly came to dominate the form. Novelists of this later century created an expanding awareness on the part of their heroes and heroines and kept the fictional experience unclosed, or open to ambiguous ethical solutions. This ambiguity is inherent in the modern experience itself with its ethical and moral contradictions. This new form became a calculated assault on the "ends" of experience, and this very shift shapes the development of Dorothy Richardson's fiction. This expansion creates an "open ended" work — and "open" refers in this sense to an ending which does not contain or "close off" the rising pressure of conscience in a novel. In a work such as *Pilgrimage* with this "open" form, the structured pattern of moral development grows broader and deeper as the novel proceeds. In spite of the obvious problems of form and structure (structural problems which Joyce solved in *Ulysses* with his focus on one day and only one day), Miss Richardson was able to create a character in Miriam Henderson whose life within the world of the novel totally dominates the work. All outward experience exerts a reciprocal pressure inward upon her innocence — this dialectic itself offering a gradual development of the character and her world. Over the course of the novel, the flux of such responses by Miriam to outward reality and her inward response not only creates and defines her character but does so through a process which the reader can isolate: Miriam is obliged to interpret herself as she interprets experience, and this double interpretative process is the primary imaginative movement in the work. The stream of responses, which is a stream of interpretation of both inner meaning and outward experience, is therefore a fundamental moral process in *Pilgrimage*. It is in this way that the reader is able to understand Miriam's experience as giving both narrative structure and ethical form to the work. As noted, the assumptions which underlie the entire concept of *Pilgrimage* are closely akin to James' theories of fiction.

It is not the intention here to discount Miss Richardson's technical contributions to the modern novel but to emphasize those larger assumptions concerning form from which emanated the development of various technical innovations in her work. The problem of controlling her material and of giving structural design to *Pilgrim-*

age was an enormous task, and one for which there had been no precedent. In attempting to create a character in a novel with an essentially "open" form and yet to give order and dimension to the work as a whole, Dorothy Richardson was trying to come to terms with one of the major problems of modern fiction. How well she accomplished this is, of course, the subject of this present study.

There are other affinities with James which are basic to Miss Richardson's fiction; her work is very much a part of that distinctive branch of modern British fiction which has its roots in James. For example, she adhered very closely to his principle of "selection" (a discussion of this concept will be taken up shortly). It was not, however, until the middle "chapters" of *Pilgrimage* that she perfected James' idea of "selection," although she follows this principle in *Pointed Roofs*. Her fiction also owes much to the Imagists and resembles closely Henri Bergson's theories of *la durée* and "pure memory." The influence of Bergson is not so direct as that of James and the Imagists, but probably came through her interest in Proust. Bergson's ideas were making an impact, however indirect, on writers at the turn of the century; and Miss Richardson's ideas of perceptions which are sharpened by memory and association have their philosophical parallels in Bergson. Miss Richardson viewed reality as subjective and believed that felt experience was real experience. In a letter to Shiv K. Kumar she writes, "I was never consciously aware of any specific influence. . . ." No doubt Bergson influenced many minds, if only by putting into words something then dawning within the human consciousness: an increased sense of the inadequacy of the clock as a time measurer.[2]

Although *Pilgrimage* is written far outside the sphere of the Imagist school of poetry, it is not outside the Imagist influence. The direction of *Pilgrimage* reflects the unclouded rhetoric of an Imagist poem. T. E. Hulme's idea of communication between human beings only by means of images seems to be inherent in the work. Miriam constantly relates her experience and thoughts in a way similar to the Imagist poem. Her images are not mere ornaments but exist in themselves. The closest parallel is in the idea that the Imagist holds of the image; it is a moment of revealed truth rather than a structure of consecutive events or thought.

To take one woman through two thousand pages of text and to maintain a single point of view is a monumental task. To compound the problem the heroine, although an interesting and mystical young woman, is rather difficult to live with for twenty-two years. The esthetic justification for the structure of the novel comes out of a necessity to create a woman in the process of becoming rather than as a character who is in a state of being. Throughout the novel, the reader views experience only through Miriam or as Miriam; and this narrow point of view which Dorothy Richardson maintained, with its severely limited and undeviating attitude toward her theme, is her debt to Henry James. Miss Richardson takes point of view beyond James in that she never deviates from the single perspective throughout *Pilgrimage*. The material itself is not arranged from a specific point of view; only the way in which Miriam experiences life remains constant; and she, like time itself, is continually changing. Her life is a life of the mind, but it is not one of contemplation.

II   *Literary Reputation*

Pointed Roofs, the first "chapter" of *Pilgrimage*, was rejected in 1913 by the publisher; but, when it finally appeared in 1915, it awakened an interest on the part of many readers and reviewers because of its *avant-garde* nature. As subsequent parts of *Pilgrimage* appeared, however, it continued to puzzle critics and readers alike; and it suffered the worst failure of *avant-garde* fiction — it remained *avant-garde*. Early reviewers made a great deal of the stream-of-consciousness technique which was employed throughout *Pilgrimage;* but the appearance of twelve separate parts of one novel between 1915 and 1938 produced a great deal of confusion.[3] By the 1930s, *Pilgrimage* seemed to be a novel with no end; and the technical innovations and the seemingly amorphous structure of the long work no longer attracted critical interest. Acceptance of Dorothy Richardson's work took a long time, but a period is not necessarily long in the historical assessment of literary reputations.

It has been over sixty years since *Pointed Roofs* was published. The recent reissue of the Knopf edition of *Pilgrimage* and its reception indicate a sustained if small interest in the work; but, while Joyce and Virginia Woolf have achieved a firm place in modern literature, Miss Richardson's modest achievement remained hardly accounted for until recently. However, with the new publication of *Pilgrimage*, the individual book-length studies by Caesar Blake and Horace Gregory, and the important bibliographical and biographical work of Gloria Glikin, Miss Richardson's reputation seems more secure and her modest contribution to modern fiction made more evident. Blake, Gregory, and Glikin have all demonstrated that Miss Richardson's treatment of feminine themes and her technical accomplishments represented important developments in English fiction.

Actually, the development of secondary material surrounding the work of Miss Richardson has been quite traditional, even in its relatively late arrival. The pattern appears to arrive in the following stages: (1) initial puzzlement on the part of the reviewers upon publication of the first chapters of *Pilgrimage*, but curiosity sustained the initial interest; (2) a gradual but pronounced decline in interest on the part of the reviewers and thus the reading public; (3) the gradual classification of her work as experimental and *avant-garde;* (4) general apathy except for a footnote in literary histories of the early twentieth century and a short but interesting study by J. C. Powys written in 1931; (5) an awakening interest in her work within the context of the modern psychological novel by Leon Edel and Robert Humphrey, who are the essential critics at this stage; (6) the individual studies by Caesar Blake and Horace Gregory were published ten years apart which is significant; (7) the new publication of the complete *Pilgrimage*, with the posthumous chapter *March Moonlight*, brings her work back into print and the relatively wide coverage by the reviewers brought her name and work back before the general reading public; and, (8) finally, the forthcoming biographical study by Gloria Glikin, part of which has been published (see bibliography), will complete a slow but definite emergence of Dorothy Richardson's reputation. More recently, John Rosenberg has written a critical biography which was published after this study was completed. Recognition was painfully slow and especially so for the author herself who lived until 1957 thinking that her work had fallen into oblivion, but this reaction was not a new feeling; she was aware throughout her literary career of the risk she was taking because of her insistence upon her personal concepts of fiction and its presentation of the feminine psyche.

III   Pointed Roofs — *The Beginning*

Miriam Henderson begins her long pilgrimage in *Pointed Roofs* as a seventeen-year-old girl who is forced by family financial circumstances to leave not only her sisters Eve, Sarah, and Harriett but also her parents in order to teach English in a German boarding school for young ladies that is conducted by Fraulein Pfaff in Hanover. From the opening lines of the novel which, as Leon Edel points out, begin conventionally enough, the reader not only enters Miriam's world but is expected to enter her mind. All the experiences and events in the novel are reflected through Miriam's consciousness — except the brief passages of dialogue between Miriam and the other characters that are independent of this process. The third person is not used conventionally, but it does not constitute statements made about Miriam by the author: the third person in the novel is Miriam's consciousness itself. The first person is used when Miriam is disturbed or when Miss Richardson wishes to achieve an artistic effect. Because of this severely restricted point of view, the reader sees and feels Miriam's impressions and embarks on her journey not only with her but through her.

In *Pointed Roofs*, the first chapter of her journey begins at her home in England and ends with her leaving the railway station in Hanover and returning to England. The reader's sense of the journey is enhanced in the second paragraph of the novel by the reference to her Saratoga trunk which "stood solid and gleaming in the firelight. Tomorrow it would be taken away and she would be gone" (I, 1). On the closing page of the novel as Miriam departs for England the idea that her trip to Germany was a portion of a longer journey is symbolically reinforced by the appearance of the same Saratoga trunk. Miriam, however, is a traveler not only in the ordinary sense but also in the spiritual realm, as *Pointed Roofs* makes clear.

The structure of *Pilgrimage*, as the title suggests, is derived from the archetypal journey or, in the more complete form, the quest. Miriam's quest is for discovery and understanding; but, as in all such journeys, conflict and struggle lie in the way. The selective process of events in *Pointed Roofs* is quite apparent; for, like Joyce's technique in *A Portrait of the Artist as a Young Man*, the scenes of Miriam's days at the school in Hanover are highly concentrated, and each is used to evoke essential experiences on the part of Miriam. By the use of this highly selective and concentrated process, the cumulative experience of these events focuses more sharply on the characters than on the events themselves, precisely the same effect Joyce achieves with Stephen Dedalus in *A Portrait*.

The trip to Germany represents for Miriam her first real independence; it becomes for her a journey into life. Despite the many doubts she has about her own ability, she is determined to make a life for herself. The financial plight of her family and her father's pride and the impact of both on her are revealed during the scene in Chapter 2 at the embarkation point in Holland where she is accompanied by her father and where they encounter a Dutchman:

"Very good, very good," she heard him say, "fine education in German schools."

Both men were smoking cigars.

She wanted to draw herself upright and shake out her clothes.

"Select," she heard, "excellent staff of masters . . . daughters of gentlemen."

Pater is trying to make the Dutchman think I am being taken as a pupil to a finishing school in Germany. She thought of her lonely pilgrimage to the West End agency, of her humiliating interview, of her heart-sinking acceptance of the post, the excitements and misgivings she had had, of her sudden challenge of them all that evening after dinner, and their dismay and remonstrance and reproaches — of her fear and determination in insisting and carrying her point and making them begin to be interested in her plan.

But she shared her father's satisfaction in impressing the Dutchman. (I, 27)

Although Miriam has been able to convince her family that she should go to Germany, she has grave self-doubts: "It was a fool's errand. . . . To undertake to go to the German school and teach . . . to be going there . . . with nothing to give" (I, 29; ellipses in text).

Miriam is not long at the school before she discovers that she is quite capable of teaching the students. Her new feeling of confidence and of adequacy as a teacher working with students increases her enjoyment of Germany. She muses over the differences between the Germans she has met in Germany and tutors in German whom she had had in England, and she is preoccupied with the differences between England and Germany in architecture and church design. In these random observations, Miriam's sensibilities emerge, especially her ability to judge distinctions of culture.

An early scene in the novel illustrates Miss Richardson's technique in bringing out Miriam's experiences and impressions. Miriam accompanies one of her students, Minna, to the oculist — a task which she abhors. Minna must submit to a series of small operations on her eyes. The depressing atmosphere of the small, faded room with its dull, coarse curtains is brought sharply into focus and is conveyed entirely through Miriam's direct sensory impressions:

The room was densely saturated with an odour which she guessed to be that of stale cigar-smoke. It seemed so tangible in the room that she looked about at first for visible signs of its presence. It was like an invisible dry fog and seemed to affect her breathing.

Coming and going upon the dense staleness of the room and pervading the immediate premises was a strange savoury pungency. Miriam could not at first identify it. But as the visits multiplied and she noticed the same odour standing in faint patches here and there about the stairways and corridors of the block, it dawned upon her that it must be onions — onions freshly frying but with a quality of accumulated richness that she could not explain. (I, 86 - 87)

After this description, Miriam contrasts this atmosphere with that of an oculist whom she had once visited on Harley Street in London: "His stately house, the exquisite freshness of his appointments and her person stood out now" (I, 87). Scenes such as these not only awaken Miriam's sense of difference in the two countries and increase her awareness of the present but also make her past more meaningful. The young Miriam is not yet ready for large philosophical and cultural distinctions; she is, however, quite capable of seeing beyond her immediate experience and of attaching significance to it. She is ecstatic about her new venture and is fully absorbed in her new life. In this first chapter of *Pilgrimage*, there is a foreshadowing of her later mysticism; she experiences moments of psychic well-being which she wonders if those around her share. When she listens to Chopin's "Fifteenth Nocturne," the music transports her into a rhapsodic state: "Everything was growing brighter and brighter. She felt that she was looking at nothing and yet was aware of the whole room like a picture in a dream. Fear left her. The human forms all round her lost their power" (I, 43). Caesar Blake suggests that "the reader is somewhat nonplused to share this kind of reaction . . . ,"[4] but he is prepared for Miriam's feeling because of her earlier reactions to people and places. Later in the long novel, the reader will find these mystical withdrawals more difficult to comprehend.

As Miriam's year in Germany passes, she becomes fond of her pupils and enjoys their company although she is often exasperated by their constant chatter and small talk. In spite of her new confidence and independence, she is still a young girl who at times longs for home and who resents her family's financial collapse: "It was cruel, cruel that she was not going to wear her blouses at home, at the tennis club . . . with Harriett" (I, 112; ellipses in text). But the most significant experience for Miriam is her friendship with Pastor Lahmann that results in Fraulein Pfaff's jealousy which leads Miriam's headmistress, the Fraulein, to send her home to England. The young girl meets Pastor Lahmann just after she has returned from a delightful walk in the "rain-sprinkled streets" of Hanover. From the moment she meets him, she recognizes a kindred spirit:

"Pastor Lahmann was standing near one of the windows. The rush of her entry carried her to the middle of the room and he met her there, smiling quietly. She stared easily and comfortably up into his great mild eyes, went into them as they remained quietly and gently there, receiving her" (I, 127). In the ensuing dialogue, Miriam and the Pastor establish an immediate rapport; but when their conversation is interrupted by Fraulein Pfaff, Miriam quickly senses or imagines the Fraulein's jealousy. After this scene, Miriam's relationship with her quickly deteriorates.

Miriam's encounter with Pastor Lahmann in a later scene reveals a great deal of Dorothy Richardson's technical artistry and affords the reader a greater insight into Miriam for the human situation in this encounter is subtly rendered. Since the reader must view the situations only through Miriam's consciousness if the consistent point of view is to be maintained and if, at the same time, the atmosphere of the scene is to be conveyed indirectly, Miss Richardson must establish a technical device appropriate for rendering the proper emotion. As the circumstances of the scene unfold, it becomes clear that the emotion cannot be conveyed by the spoken word, nor can Miriam's limited point of view convey the full effect of the scene. It is through the eyes of the participants that the mood is carried to the reader; and, although Miriam is the sentient character, the eye symbol gives the reader an air of dramatic detachment. Pastor Lahmann's eyes are described as "great mild eyes." As Miriam looked at Pastor Lahmann,

She felt her gaze growing fixed and moved to withdraw it and herself.
"Why do you wear glasses, mademoiselle?"
The voice was full of sympathetic wistfulness. "I have a severe myopic astigmatism," she announced, gathering up her music and feeling the words as little hammers on the newly seen, pallid, rounded face.
"You wear them always — for how long?"
"Poor child, poor child, and you must have passed through all your schooling with those lame, lame eyes . . . let me see the eyes . . . turn a little to the light . . . so." [Ellipses in text]
Standing near and large he scrutinized her vague gaze.
"And sensitive to light, too." (I, 129)

After the dialogue has been interrupted by the Fraulein, Miriam is at first pleased "at the thought of being grouped with him in the *eyes* of Fraulein Pfaff" (I, 129, italics mine). Fraulein Pfaff's eyes are ab-

sent from the scene because she is clearly the outsider. The symbol
of the eyes is expanded and deepened in a later scene with the Pastor
and the Fraulein. E. K. Brown has written that the "expanding symbol responds to the impulses of the novelist who is aware that he cannot give us the core of his meaning, but strains to reveal now this
aspect of it, now that aspect, in a sequence of sudden flashes."[5] And
in precisely this way Miss Richardson overcomes the technical difficulties inherent in conveying the proper mood of these two scenes.

In the second circumstance, the same three are riding in a brake
through the German countryside; Miriam is sitting next to her friend
Emma across from Pastor Lahmann and Fraulein Pfaff. As she sits
directly opposite him and enjoys the beauty of the evening, Miriam
thinks to herself "that only he could feel the beauty of the evening
exactly as she did" (I, 159). Her mind begins to dwell on the spiritual
union she has with him: "Several times she met and quietly contemplated his dark eyes. She felt that there was someone in those
eyes who was neither tiresome nor tame. She was looking at someone
to whom those boys and that dead wife were nothing. At first he had
met her eyes formally, then with obvious embarrassment, and at last
simply and gravely. She felt easy and happy in this communion" (I,
156 - 57).

Just as Miriam's eyes and Pastor Lahmann's evoke a spiritual communion, Miriam looks over at Fraulein Pfaff and sees in her eyes
"disgust and loathing." The eyes, depending upon the beholder, can
convey either love or hate; and through this organ many of Miriam's
insights develop. The Platonic idea of the eyes as the windows of the
soul is clearly echoed in both scenes; and, just as in John Donne's
poem "The Canonization," the eyes afford a spiritual communion
between Miriam and Pastor Lahmann. By using this symbol, the
author is able to achieve the dramatic effect intended and, at the
same time, remain consistent in her point of view.

Despite her falling out with Fraulein Pfaff, Miriam, when spring
comes, is totally absorbed in and mystified by the beauties of Germany that surround her. The people and places have new meanings
for her, and she feels secure in knowing that the girls at the school
like her and feel attached to her. Her teaching continues to go well
in spite of her disagreements with Fraulein Pfaff, but the Fraulein
finally tells her that she must leave in spite of her success. Her first,
reactions are to look back at her year as one of defeat; but, underlying her unhappiness, she has a growing awareness of her independence and freedom. Fraulein Pfaff becomes the first an-

tagonist and the conflict in the heroine's quest for selfhood; for Miriam sees her as an authority figure. While Miriam is associated with spring and light, the Fraulein, the antagonist, is associated with winter, darkness, sterility, and old age.[6] All of these impressions are developed through this highly concentrated imagistic rendering. These impressions develop cumulatively through the use of recurring images and the rhythm which they establish.

Miriam's long, discursive self-incriminations earlier in the novel and her later euphoria seem to lack emotional power; but they are important, even though tiresome, because these self-examinations, while oftentimes superficial, give the reader a great deal of insight into Miriam's nature and form important ideas related to her later development. At times, her fleeting thoughts are the typical idealism of an adolescent, no doubt a very sensitive one. At one point, she thinks "she felt sure she ought to discuss with the girls . . . improving the world . . . leaving it better than you found it . . . the importance of life" (I, 95, ellipses in text). Miss Richardson makes a heavy demand upon the reader's ability to concentrate as the shifting images of Miriam's year in Germany filter through the highly impressionistic mind of the heroine. There is no problem of suspension of belief on the part of the reader; it is rather a problem of maintaining the troublesome discipline of having to view all phenomena within the novel through the consciousness of a seventeen-year-old girl as she lives her first experience away from home.

It has been noted that in plot and structure *Pointed Roofs* appears to be a departure from the traditional British novel of the late nineteenth or early twentieth century; and this work is certainly different from the fiction of John Galsworthy and Arnold Bennett, for example. From the beginning, the reader is aware of the author's search for a more intense way of bringing a character's experience to the reader that conventional forms of the novel did not provide. Admittedly, plot is seen differently in the 1970s, but *Pointed Roofs* represented a radical departure from the traditional concepts of plot held in 1915. *Pointed Roofs* is not without plot even in the more traditional sense of the term. Plot, of course, is ancillary to the design of the whole, but it is not absent. Young Miriam, forced by financial circumstances and a sense of independence, pursues a career and embarks on a teaching position in Germany; and, during her stay, she learns a great deal about herself and is puzzled by her reactions. Because of a friendship with Pastor Lahmann which is only a culmination of a series of differences with the headmistress of the school, she is forced to return to England. Plot is certainly there; but it is merely relegated to a less important place in the shaping of the novel. Miriam knits together a chain of events, but the events are only important insofar as they affect her being; and, in a stream-of-consciousness novel, the concern is with the consciousness rather than with the external action. Thus, the reader has the advantage of being able to view Miriam's reaction in a way in which she herself cannot.

Characters appear, but their importance is dependent upon Miriam. Events take place, but, again, the importance of them is only in their relationship to Miriam and what she chooses to make of them. The structural unity of the entire novel is dependent, therefore, upon the single character and the journey. In short, Miss Richardson illustrates in abundance those aspects of fiction which Henry James proclaimed as most significant. Miriam is the center of conscience, the sensitive character through whom all the moral considerations are filtered.

One might concur that *Pointed Roofs* as it stands alone lacks complication and resolution in the conventional sense, that it is just one "chapter" in the larger design of *Pilgrimage; Pointed Roofs* is only the story of Miriam's beginning on her long journey through time and space, the first "chapter" within the structural framework of a long psychological novel. *Pointed Roofs*, however, is of great importance in its relationship to the whole of *Pilgrimage:* it was not intended to stand apart and cannot be treated exclusively as a single novel because of its intricate position in the development of the whole. As one reads subsequent chapters, the technical mastery in *Pilgrimage* increases; and the nature of Miriam's experience is more complex and involved. *Pointed Roofs* introduces the reader to Miriam; but, more important, it also introduces most of the major themes of *Pilgrimage.* Not only does the reader meet Miriam and become aware of the subleties of her personality and sensibilities, he is made aware of the technical devices that the author employs and her Bergsonian sense of time. The themes of mysticism, feminism, and freedom which dominate the later "chapters" come into focus in *Pointed Roofs* and are given more definite shape in the later works that comprise *Pilgrimage.*

The style, too, changes as *Pilgrimage* progresses. *Pointed Roofs* is told in the past tense; on the other hand, *March Moonlight,* the last "chapter," is predominantly rendered in the present. This shift in tense is paralleled by the change from the third-person narration of

Pointed Roofs to the first person in *March Moonlight*. At this point, author and character merge; and action or thought is related simultaneously with its occurrence: "While I write, everything vanishes but what I contemplate. The whole of what is called 'the past' is with me, seen anew, vividly. No, Schiller, the past does not stand 'being still.' It moves, growing with one's growth. Contemplation is adventure into discovery; reality. What is called 'creation,' imaginative transformation, fantasy, invention, is only based on reality" (IV, 657). These lines indicate the degree to which the technique itself in *Pilgrimage* is constantly undergoing change; this evolution, however, is gradual and reflects the long years of composition; nevertheless, the change is evident from "chapter" to "chapter" within *Pilgrimage*.

The foregoing remarks have admittedly stressed those aspects of *Pointed Roofs* which seem to break with earlier traditions in the English novel, but it should also be noted that very much of this first section is shaped within and continuous with the development of the English novel. For example, as Horace Gregory has noted,

The literary roots of *Pilgrimage* are decisively English, and are to be found in the writings of Charlotte Bronte: *Pointed Roofs* runs parallel to Bronte's *Villette:* the same fictional-autobiographical design is apparent in both; in both the heroine is a very young, unskilled instructress in a continental girls' school, the Bronte school in Belgium, the Richardson school in Germany. In *Pilgrimage* we are not surprised to find its heroine, Miriam, with a much-read copy of *Villette* in her hand. Her temperament is very like that of its heroine, Lucy Snowe. She has the same quality of passionate conviction in her opinions, the same English honesty, the same unshrewdness, the same wholeheartedness that define Lucy's character. Which is to say that *Pilgrimage* belongs to the tradition of English Romantic fiction in which the Bronte sisters were forerunners of their kind.[7]

Gregory's points are well taken, and they also stress what is so often taken for granted or ignored by the critic who writes about a literary figure such as Dorothy Richardson. The experimentalist owes much to the tradition from which he breaks, which is certainly true of Miss Richardson's art.

IV   Backwater — *The First Return*

Backwater begins with Miriam back home in England ready to assume a new teaching position for the Misses Perne in London. There is no attempt on the part of the author to give an outline of the chronology, as she did in *Pointed Roofs*, by selecting the important experiences throughout the school year and tying them in with the school and seasonal calendar. Miriam's experiences are still broken down into impressions which constantly merge into one another, but the conceptions are kept from complete dissolution by the strict consistency of the point of view which keeps the flux of events and impressions constantly in Miriam's consciousness.

The story opens with an account of Miriam's interview with the three sisters who conduct the school in North London, Banbury Park. Miriam is displeased with her mother for "piling it on" during the interview — an act which recalls her father's remarks to the Dutchman on their trip to Germany. As she and her mother travel through London, Miriam is intrigued by the movement of the city and its people; and she becomes quickly attuned to her new life and approaches it in the same mystical way in which she did Hanover:

The people passing along them were unlike any she knew. There were no ladies, no gentlemen, no girls or young men such as she knew. They were all alike. They were . . . She could find no word for the strange impression they made. It coloured the whole of the district through which they had come. It was part of the new world to which she was pledged to go on September 18th. It was her world already; and she had no words for it. She would not be able to convey it to others. . . . She must deal with it alone. . . . It was her secret. A strange secret for all her life as Hanover had been. (I, 195)

After her interview in London, Miriam returns home, shares briefly in the domestic life with her sisters, and smokes her first cigarette as an act of independence and rebellion against prescribed social behavior. At a dance, she ignores her friend Ted in order to seek the company of Max who hums "Lorelei" and understands German. Miriam has a long conversation in the garden with Max until Ted interrupts them and asks, "Aren't you *ever* going to dance with me again?" (I, 223). The scenes are bland; they lack the dramatic power and richness of a provincial scene which Jane Austen could create so well; and they are also devoid of her remarkable irony. But Miss Richardson's scenes reveal Miriam's awareness of men and the inferior relationship women have to them in English society.

Miss Richardson is able to avoid the technical hazards which often result in a lack of clarity of presentation when only such a narrow point of view is used. The dialogue between Max and Miriam rings true as they talk in the garden. Because Ted finds them together, he leaves the party and breaks off his relationship with her; but Miriam is quickly reconciled to this situation and anticipates the new teaching position in London.

She enjoys the young girls just as she did in Hanover, and her time is filled with teaching, teas, and conversation. But she begins to take on a double life, for she starts reading late into the night — a great deal of fiction — and is intrigued with Robert Burton's *Anatomy of Melancholy*. Her mind begins to speculate about such political ideas as press censorship and *laissez-faire*, which she calls "Lazy Fair." She reads voraciously, but her mental turmoil over religion which began in *Pointed Roofs* increases and is complicated by the Pernes who take it upon themselves to increase her piety. As time goes on at the Pernes' school, Miriam reaches near despair; at one point, she contemplates the nature of death and recalls an experience that occurred when she was a child. She remembers waking up on her seventh birthday and saying to herself that one day her mother and father would die, and she would be all alone. Perhaps a more revealing recollection at this point is an incident in which she looked out of a dining room window at Barnes where "the raindrops were falling from the leaves through the sunshine and saying to Eve, 'D' you know, Eve, I feel as if I'd suddenly wakened up out of a dream" (I, 245).

At this point, Miriam is in a crucial stage of her development; for she is developing from her loneliness and introspection not only her attitudes toward society but her place in it. Her isolation is an attempt to understand life, but solitude no longer affords her a pleasant withdrawal. She is becoming increasingly aware that there is a truth to be arrived at not socially or intellectually, but personally, intuitively, imaginatively, through impressions, images, and symbols. As the title implies, this period is clearly a bleak one; and the reader is able to see a definite contrast in mood from the pleasant days in Hanover to the bleakness of the heroine's year in North London.

Miriam's probing into experience and meaning takes on greater depth as she tries to untangle the mysteries of life which surround her. There is a growing desire on her part to be alone, but she realizes that this isolation is not enough; conflicts emerge. She knows that simply "to get away somewhere by herself every day would not be enough. If that were all she could have, there would come a time when there would be nothing anywhere" (I, 279 - 80). As her perceptions become more acute and her depression increases, the moments of euphoric bliss which came upon her in Hanover disappear. Her loneliness and yearning are now much more deeply rooted than they were; her sense of being ignored by time becomes paramount. One afternoon, while walking in the park, she sees the figure of a man coming toward her:

For a moment her heart cried out to him. If he would come straight on and, understanding, would walk into her life and she could face this knowing that he was there, the light would come back and would stay until the end — and there would be other lives, on and on. She stood transfixed, trembling. He grew more and more distinct and she saw a handbag and the outline of a bowler hat; a North London clerk hurrying home to tea. With bent head she turned away and dragged her shamed heavy limbs rapidly towards home. (I, 280)

As her needs increase, Miriam finds herself getting farther and farther away from the light which she had found earlier in times of happiness. For her, light has become a mystic symbol for revelation and truth. This truth which she seeks is attached to an intuitive understanding of life; these moments of illumination which provide her with the light are becoming more complex, for she is beginning to attach more and more meaning to these intensified glimpses of reality.

Her mystical experience in *Backwater* reaches its climax early in the novel as she is walking up the staircase which results in a flash of truth that provides her with a deeper understanding of herself.

If you were not wanted. . . . If you knew you were not wanted — you ought to get out of the way. Chloroform. Someone had drunk a bottle of carbolic acid. The clock struck ten . . . she . . . went slowly upstairs, watching the faint reflection of the half lowered hall gas upon the polished balustrade. The staircase was cold and airy. Cold rooms and landings stretched up above her into the darkness. She became aware of a curious buoyancy rising within her. It was so strange that she stood still for a moment on the stair. For a second life seemed to cease in her and the staircase to be swept from under her feet. . . . 'I'm alive.' . . . It was as if something had struck her, struck her right through her impalpable body, sweeping it away, leaving her shouting silently without it. I'm alive. . . . I'm alive. Then with a thump her heart went on again and her feet carried her body, warm and happy and elastic, easily on up the solid stairs. She tried once or twice deliberately to bring back the breathless moment standing still on a stair. Each time something of it returned. It's me, *me;* this is *me* being alive.' . . . (I, 244 - 45)

The motif of the staircase is woven into the entire fabric of *Pilgrimage.* In Freudian psychology the climbing of the staircase is a traditional symbol for the sexual act; but, as Miss Richardson uses it, it seems to be without the usual Freudian convolutions. But, when connected with the Freudian idea that the sexual act can lead to illumination, there is perhaps a parallel. Miriam's many trips up and down stairs throughout the book are usually accompanied by light. At the opening of the novel, Miriam "left the gaslit hall and went slowly upstairs. The March twilight lay upon the landings, but the staircase was almost dark. The top was quite dark and silent" (I, 15). At the beginning of her journey, she is not aware of the nature of her search; and her quest is shrouded in darkness and "twilight." In the later staircase episodes, light plays an increasing role in the imagery which surrounds her ascents of the staircase.

As Maisel has suggested, the Freudian interpretation of a staircase as a symbol for the sexual act may not be altogether irrelevant if one remembers the lack of explicit sexual reference in the work. "But has not ascent, the penetration of the real as in the Biblical story of the ladder going up, always been one of the mystic's chief symbols?"[8] As Miriam becomes more and more aware of her ability to perceive truth intuitively, an increasing radiance surrounds her upward ascents on the staircases throughout *Pilgrimage*. Since her journey is in many ways a mystical quest, the Biblical idea of the upward ladder seems to be symbolically related to the many ascents. The pattern of these mystical ascents is established from the opening lines in *Pointed Roofs*, and it gradually evolves in subsequent episodes throughout the novel. In *The Tunnel*, the mystical journey motif is reinforced in its connection with the staircase in the third paragraph: "Assuring Mrs. Bailey that she remembered the way to the room, she started at last on the journey up the many flights of stairs" (II, 11). The staircase symbolism functions as a unifying motif throughout Miriam's journey.

Backwater reveals more fully a technique which was not so apparent in *Pointed Roofs* but which becomes a major design throughout *Pilgrimage*: the use of the recurring image as a structural design and as a method for character revelation. For example, Miriam's quest for fulfillment and meaning manifests itself often in *Backwater* through recurring images of white light or brightness; and her sense of stagnation is frequently expressed in the metaphor of a veil, a block which allows her a glimpse of a deeper and more meaningful life, but, nevertheless, separates her from that life:

One day she left the pathways and strayed amongst pools of shadow lying under the great trees. As she approached the giant trunks and the detail of their shape and colour grew clearer her breathing quickened. She felt her prim bearing about her like a cloak. The reality she had found was leaving her again. Looking up uneasily into the forest of leaves above her head she found them strange. She walked quickly back into the sunlight, gazing reproachfully at the trees. There they were as she had always known them; but between them and herself was her governess's veil, close drawn, holding them sternly away from her. (I, 279)

In the scene immediately following, Miriam thinks of her experience at the German school and at Banbury Park and is reassured: "And the discovery that it was not dead, that her six months in the German school and the nine long months during which Banbury Park life had drawn a veil even over the little slices of holiday freedom, had not even touched it, brought her warm moments of reassurance" (I, 282).

These references to the veil, along with the multiple references to trams and their movement, support the overall metaphor of the imprisonment, the stagnation, and the near despair which form the essential mood of *Backwater*, as the title itself insists. More important, however, these metaphors and recurring images support the thematic elements in the novel and also help to define Miriam's psychic condition; and, in so doing, they add depth and dimension to her character and still keep the singularity of point of view.

V *Interior Monologue and Form*

Before going farther with the analysis of *Pilgrimage*, interior monologue technique and several of the underlying assumptions present in Dorothy Richardson's novel should be considered. It is apparent from the discussion thus far that Miss Richardson, like Virginia Woolf, was an experimenter, an esthetic radical; and, since she believed that ordinary life must be given the form of art, she was far more interested in the overall texture and its verbal modes of unity than in the total structure of *Pilgrimage*. The esthetic logic of the novel is achieved as much by a variety of rhetorical strategies as by the processes of human interaction and meditation on the part of the heroine, Miriam Henderson. Perhaps the most common device besides the use of recurring images and other referential literary devices which develop spatiality in the work is the use of the stream-of-consciousness technique. Although much has been written about this method, the concern of the authors has been primarily about Joyce and Virginia Woolf.

Indeed, May Sinclair was the first one to use William James' term to apply to Miss Richardson's work when she wrote an appreciation of the first three parts of *Pilgrimage:*

To me these three novels show an art and method and form carried to punctilious perfection. . . . In this series there is no drama, no situation, no set scene. Nothing happens. It is just life going on and on. It is Miriam Henderson's stream of consciousness going on and on. . . . In identifying herself with this life, which is Miriam's stream of consciousness, Miss Richardson produces her effect of being the first, of getting closer to reality than any of our novelists who are trying so desperately to get close.[9]

Dorothy Richardson herself could not abide the term: "What do I think of the term 'Stream of Consciousness' as applied, in England, to the work of several modern novelists? Just this: that amongst the company of useful labels devised to meet the exigencies of literary criticism it stands alone, isolated by its perfect imbecility. The transatlantic amendment, 'Interior Monologue,' though rather more inadequate than even a label has any need to be, at least carries a meaning."[10] The metaphor of the "stream" is rejected by Miss Richardson, for she ridicules the term as flowery. It remains, for her, stable: "But his [man's] consciousness sits stiller than a tree. . . . tho more or less continuously expanding from birth to maturity, remains stable, one with itself throughout life."[11] Consciousness is thus viewed by Miss Richardson in spatial terms rather than in terms of time. The term, stream-of-consciousness, for her, in other words, was phenomenologically incorrect, for the human consciousness expanded with time but remained stable and was not, like a stream, in constant flux. Given this serious question which Miss Richardson has raised concerning the phrase, the term "Interior Monologue" should be used in this study out of respect both for her logic and for her work.

When one sees Miriam in those moments of illumination, one is not dealing merely with the patented aspects of the high points in her personal history, thought, and language but also with the recurring images toward which Miriam inclines in articulating experience and which enrich the woven pattern of her mind. The unity of texture in these images of light, spring, the staircase, and other recurring ones not only recall earlier passages to the reader but prepare him for future ones. The structural patterns provided by the author through her technique and her use of recurring images give *Pil-*

grimage the unities of space and time, expansion as well as movement. Robert Humphrey in his book *Stream of Consciousness in the Modern Novel* writes that "the stream of consciousness fiction which relies most on imagery is Dorothy Richardson's *Pilgrimage.*"[12] To Humphrey, Miss Richardson describes the impressions which Miriam has with imagery rather than with narrative; and this technique is handled so skillfully that the reader is able "to identify images with certain moods of the character, and he comes to be able to fill in the blank spaces in Miriam's own private psyche."[13]

Since Miss Richardson completely identifies herself with Miriam, the omniscience is confined to Miriam. The use of the third-person description seems rather conventional at first until the reader begins to realize that, although the novel is presented from the focal point of the all-knowing author, the omniscience never goes beyond Miriam's consciousness. This technique, which enhances the singleness of the point of view, involves, however, two methods of interior monologue that are used in *Pilgrimage*. The first is the description which is no different in outward appearance from the conventional third-person description except that the author and character are inseparable; the second method is that of direct interior monologue. The closing paragraph of *Honeycomb* offers an excellent illustration of the two techniques:

The bony old woman held Miriam clasped closely in her arms. "You must never, as long as you live, blame yourself, my gurl." She went away. Miriam had not heard her come in. The pressure of her arms and her huge body came from far away. Miriam clasped her hands together. She could not feel them. Perhaps she had dreamed that the old woman had come in and said that. Everything was dream; the world. I shall not have any life. I can never have any life; all my days. There were cold tears running into her mouth. They had no salt. Cold water. They stopped. Moving her body with slow difficulty against the unsupporting air, she looked slowly about. It was so difficult to move. Everything was airy and transparent. Her heavy hot light impalpable body was the only solid thing in the world, weighing tons; and like a lifeless feather. There was a tray of plates of fish and fruit on the table. She looked at it, heaving with sickness and looking at it. I am hungry. Sitting down near it she tried to pull the tray. It would not move. I must eat the food. Go on eating food, till the end of my life. Plates of food like these plates of food. . . . I am in eternity . . . where their worm dieth not and their fire is not quenched. (I, 489 - 90; ellipses in text)

As the paragraph begins, the narration is straight third person. The first eight sentences and their organization and structure reflect the activity of Miriam's mind. These sentences describe what surrounds her, but each one brings the reader increasingly closer to Miriam's consciousness, and the last sentence in the third person goes directly into her mind ("Perhaps she had dreamed that the old woman had come in and said that.") Then, smoothly, the paragraph goes into interior monologue; and, after the ninth sentence which acts as a transitional one, the pronoun shifts to "I"; the reader is directly in Miriam's consciousness; and the third person narration is dropped. Then, just as smoothly, the narrator returns again and then fades out; and the closing sentences take us directly back to Miriam's consciousness through interior monologue. These two methods are fused so adroitly within the paragraph that the reader is not distracted by the change of methods. The effect of this shift is somewhat cinematic and is similar to the fade-out technique used by the cameraman. The reader soon realizes the direct method is used only in moments of intensity, and the shift enhances the dramatic effectiveness. Unlike earlier psychological novelists such as Henry James, Dorothy Richardson's method is descriptive rather than analytical. The elements of her psychic consciousness are sense elements, and they remain so throughout the novel.

VI *Saturation versus Selection*

Horace Gregory has maintained that the influence of H. G. Wells on Dorothy Richardson "was practical and personal as well as literary."[14] He also accounts for the reasons why Wells' influence has been underestimated:

Earlier discussions of *Pilgrimage* have associated Dorothy Richardson's name almost exclusively with the "stream of consciousness" novel, and in these discussions mention of Wells seems an irrelevance. In spite of its title, his *Experiment in Autobiography* was not the work of an experimental novelist; and he carried with him no claims of being an artist. Another reason why Wells's relationship to Dorothy Richardson has received less notice than it should is the decline of his literary reputation. Obliquely, the fall cast a shadow across the last years of Dorothy Richardson's life when her own reputation had slipped to its lowest ebb. The later years of Wells's long and influential career were wasted in his devotion to journalism — so much so that his last image to the public was one of H. G. Wells who had become not unlike Lewis Carroll's "man dressed in newspapers." Even today, almost twenty years after his death, evaluation of his worth lacks perspective and balance. During the years of his greatest fame he was overpraised to the same degree that he is underestimated today.

A third reason why the distance between Wells and Dorothy Richardson

seems greater than it is, is that many historians and critics have overlooked
the fact that the "makers" of the new English novel between 1890 and 1920
had been welcomed or rejected either as "naturalists" or latter-day
"realists."[15]

In spite of this argument, Gregory himself clearly notes that Dorothy
Richardson "moved far beyond the example Wells provided."[16] It is
abundantly clear from her fiction that Miss Richardson was far closer
in her thinking to Henry James about problems of literary form than
to her friend H. G. Wells.

While she was composing *Pointed Roofs* and *Backwater*, a great
literary debate was raging in England between James and Wells
about the form the novel should take. James and Wells were arguing
both publicly and privately about saturation and selection.[17] Despite
her relationship with Wells, Miss Richardson's fictional technique
was similar to James'; but she felt that he was guilty of exclusion —
that, although James used the single observer, the observer's full
awareness of life was removed from him. James held that the artist
must select his material in order to avoid a mere documentation of
life rather than an artistic re-creation; and he used the term
"saturation" as synonymous with Wells' term "discursive." Wells
felt that any action which involved the character could validly be inserted in the novel as long as the mood was consistent, and his ideas
were decidedly more popular at the time. He wrote: "The distinctive
value of the novel among written works of art is in characterization,
and the charm of a well conceived character lies, not in knowing its
destiny, but in watching its proceedings."[18] With this point James
took issue because he saw the direction that the novel written in this
way was taking: looseness of focus, author intrusion, and form-
lessness. Wells also intimated that the novel was a social vehicle
and not an end in itself, a view to which James was diametrically opposed and one to which Miss Richardson certainly could never
adhere. James indicated, however, that an author really had not too
much of a choice since a novelist had to select his material even in a
novel of saturation; otherwise, he would be surrounded by an
amorphous mass which would destroy his artistic effect.

Miss Richardson's long novel becomes increasingly Jamesian in
structure. After the first three parts — *Pointed Roofs, Backwater*,
and *Honeycomb* — the subsequent "chapters" are more controlled,
centered, and selective; and her specific intention is more firmly in
mind. The actions and events which surround Miriam are centered

around a controlling purpose of structure and unity of tone and mood; but, as has been stated, this "structure" lacks the conventional sense of that word — at least, it was not conventional at the time she began *Pilgrimage* since every impression which Miriam has is increasingly more relevant to her development. In the early "chapters" of *Pilgrimage*, Dorothy Richardson was not unaware of James' view of selection since she had very early in her career admired his point-of-view strategy; she perfected her technique as the work grew. The two opposing views of the novel which James and Wells carried on inevitably influenced Miss Richardson, and she took her direction from James just as she had in other issues because she found it more suitable to the kind of fiction she was writing. As a result, her Miriam adheres to the Jamesian concept of the intelligent, introspective character who is the sensitive, the reflective, and the "intelligent center" of consciousness for the entire novel and who is the proper focus of the whole.

VII *Time*

The question of time has always been one of the most disturbing for the human imagination, for time has been an enemy. Modern writers have been especially concerned with the relationship of the finite in the face of the infinite. John Keats in "Ode on a Grecian Urn" expressed the dilemma of one who comes upon those idyllic moments and realizes his inability to capture and hold them as they drift endlessly away. Keats felt that those lovers who were fixed eternally on the urn had a tremendous advantage over man who was susceptible to the continual flow of time. Miss Richardson did not take the view that man was outside the flow of time; she believed that time, in so far as man is able to experience it, is highly subjective and must be understood in relationship to the self. For her, time had a flux which possessed structure and meaning; for she believed that an understanding of the self was only attainable through a penetration into the mysteries that time held for the individual. In this way, a person is able to pass through experience and become illuminated by it; but each illumination leads to another experience — and each experience leads to additional illumination. Man is changed with the lapse of each particle of a second, but the self remains even though he is subject to this temporal succession. Memory alone does not make up the entire consciousness; it is but one aspect of it.

Proust's *Remembrance of Things Past* ends in apparent triumph;

the search for the meaning of temporal succession is fulfilled. For Virginia Woolf, time is the victor: Mrs. Ramsey, the central consciousness of *To The Lighthouse* searches for a coherence, an order; but she is defeated in the end. When the trip to the lighthouse finally comes to pass, Mrs. Ramsey, thwarted by time, is dead. In the "millwheeling vicociclometer" of H. C. Earwicker's dream in *Finnegans Wake*, Joyce's metaphysical idea of time is ambivalent in that he sees a tension between the retrogressive forces of man and the rectifying force of the ideal. With this theory in mind, the reader is able to see why Joyce looked to the poet for much of his art: the poet gave meaning to the future, a center to history, and a tolerance to time. Joyce's view of time was larger than Dorothy Richardson's in that it was less individual.

The private experience of time is an essential element of Dorothy Richardson's fiction. Succession, flux, and change belong to the most immediate and primitive data of experience; and each of these aspects of time is connected to a life. No experience exists which is not without temporal attachment; but these experiences, linked in time, are not the whole of the consciousness for Miss Richardson. Her fiction enriches man's sense of time because she is able to capture in her art the terribly abstract vision of man in flux and yet stable — an anchorite in time because of the unique quality of his nature. Her fiction demanded a sense of time and also recognition of its all-importance to sensation, impressions, and experience. Her character, Miriam, is clearly aware of the distinction in time made by the Greeks: for them, the word "kairos" expressed clock time, whereas "chronos" expressed abstract time.

The most important theory of time in this century for novelists has been the idea expressed by Henri Bergson. Bergson's theory was important to novelists because he saw time as an immediate datum of consciousness as it enters the individual. His term was "duration," and he meant by it that men experience time as a continuous flow. To him, time is characterized not only by successive moments and by multiple changes but also by something which endures within succession and change. He believed that the quality of continuous flow, or duration, does not find an adequate correlate in the physical concept of time — by time such as clock time which is measured outside the individual.[19]

Shiv Kumar has argued for the close similarity between Bergson's concept of consciousness and Miss Richardson's and for Bergson's indirect influence on her. Kumar notes, however, that there is a distinction; for Miss Richardson's concept has a fixed center in the consciousness but Bergson's theory does not admit this factor. A more recent critic, Shirley Rose, argues strongly about the distinction:

The dialectic of being and becoming lies at the heart of Dorothy Richardson's aesthetics. Both she and Bergson posit a necessary core from which life flows, but for her this core is apprehensible and is the only zone where reality exists. Bergson applies the concept of apprehensible reality only to the actual, the phenomenal, the intellectual, and the products of the physical or mental energies. Dorothy Richardson would say that the inherent reality of the external world is perceptible to the consciousness through the mediation of the senses. Like James Joyce, she holds that experience contains innumerable epiphanies. Moreover, these are recognized as a result of our awareness of our own being, that is, by means of momentarily curtailing the transitory nature of certain experience in order to intuit the immutable that also lies outside ourselves.[20]

Rose cites an example of such self-awareness from *Clear Horizon* where "Miriam is emerging from what might be called a state of suspension in confronting external reality"[21]:

this strange, cold trance . . . was now asserting itself as central and permanent, and sternly suggesting that the whole of the past had been a long journey in a world of illusion. Supposing this were true, supposing this cold contemplation of reality stripped of its glamour were all that remained, there was still space in consciousness, far away behind this benumbed surface, where dwelt whatever it was that now came forward, not so much to give battle as to invite her to gather herself away from this immovable new condition and watch, from a distance, unattained, the behaviour of the newly discovered world. (IV, 296)

The consciousness itself absorbs the flow of time rather than moving with it. The gradual change in Miriam, then, as Rose so perceptively argues, is in the " 'opening of the inward eye,' the final unfolding of the consciousness to complete spatial absorption of reality, free from the linear constructs of the rational or associative faculties of the mind."[22] Reality emanates from the developing self, but the self is continuously absorbing the external and thus forming its own growth, not merely within the flow of time, but from the conscious self as it expands and grows in awareness.

The apparent chaotic impressions which come upon her and the associations which Miriam makes include not only elements from memory but also expectations; hence, since past and future are involved with the specious present, chronological time disappears. A reordering or different direction is given to time as the consciousness acts on its flow. Miriam's perceptions are a realization of things and events in space which give vitality to the past. The ideal essences of experiences and impressions in the mind of the beholder become more real than the experiences themselves. Miss Richardson's use of the memory and its place in time is much like Proust's type of memory which was a recollection of those single, unrepeatable experiences that are active in the quest for the recovery of time and yet independent of it. Joyce's theory of the epiphany corresponds with this idea as does Virginia Woolf's concept of intensified moments. Miriam's recollections later in the novel of the beauties of the *Saal* while she was in Germany, of her happier moments spent with her sisters, of the rain against the pavement in London, of those moments of discovery in the quiet of a garden, of someone's smile, and multitudes of other events serve to convey a meaning to her which could not be elicited from the contents of the immediate experience. These impressions establish a pattern for the whole and provide for a thematic unity. It is these recollections from memory and the present associations which operate on her consciousness and give meaning to her life. Miss Richardson relies upon Miriam throughout *Pilgrimage* to give the novel unity; all the material in the novel is seen from her point of view. The unity is controlled through this myriad of impressions rendered through Miriam's consciousness.

VIII   Honeycomb

Miriam's move from the world of *Backwater* into that of *Honeycomb* is a vast one. Some of the important elements in Miss Richardson's fiction have already been discussed. This novel demonstrates many of these aspects, but the basic conflicts in Miriam that came to the surface in *Backwater* are submerged until the later part of *Honeycomb*. The subject matter, of course, is presented in the same manner as the earlier chapters, but the mood is distinctly changed since Miriam's spirits are buoyed up by her new surroundings. The undercurrents of conflict, however, remain.

When *Honeycomb* opens, Miriam has left the Pernes' school because of the severe financial demands on her family which require that she earn more money. Miriam's new position as a governess for the Corries at Newlands is especially appealing to her because it enables her to be freed of the dreary atmosphere of Banbury Park that has nearly led her to despair. The opening paragraph of *Honeycomb* sets the mood of the early part of the novel, provides a smooth transition from *Backwater*, and reinforces the journey theme which shapes the entire novel:

> When Miriam got out of the train into the darkness she knew that there were woods all about her. The moist air was rich with the smell of trees — wet bark and branches — moss and lichen, damp dead leaves. She stood on the dark platform snuffing the rich air. It was the end of her journey. Anything that might follow would be unreal compared to this moment. Little bulbs of yellow light further up the platform told her where she must turn to find the things she must go to meet. "How lovely the air is here." . . . The phrase repeated itself again and again, going with her up the platform towards the group of lights. It was all she could summon to meet the new situation. It satisfied her; it made her happy. It was enough; but no one would think it was enough. (I, 349)

Light again plays an important part in the imagery surrounding her ascents during these mystical moments in her journey. Miriam will recall later that this interim is not in fact an "end of her journey"; it is a fresh beginning on her quest which will end in disillusionment. The hollow life which she finds at Newlands after she has been there for a time increases her loneliness, and her earlier conflicts become more pronounced.

As Miriam begins her position as governess for the Corries' two children at Newlands, she is immediately struck by the lavish living which contrasts with her drab life in Banbury Park. Although the Corries offer young Miriam a view of the life of a wealthy class which she had never seen, the world of superabundance in this provincial society awakens in her a social sense which remains with her long after her stay at Newlands. During her early days of tutoring and living with the family, Miriam temporarily forgets her sense of failure and depression as she is caught up in the life of the household; she becomes absorbed in her work and the natural beauties of the English countryside; she responds to the invigorating stimuli around her. These brief insights and moments of "thoughts recollected in tranquility" fill her with such a sense of well-being and fulfillment that, during the early stages of *Honeycomb*, she looks forward to her new life with expectancy: "There was a life ahead that was going to enrich and change her as she had been enriched and changed by Hanover, but much more swiftly and intimately" (I, 351). The conflicts which developed in her consciousness in *Pointed Roofs* and *Backwater* are, however, far from resolved. Miriam's ideas concerning men and religion emerge from what in the two earlier "chapters" were only half articulated thoughts or subconscious feelings.

The important events in the story concern Miriam's relationships with Mr. Corrie and Bob Greville, her dawning recognition of the superficial life at Newlands, the impending marriages of her sisters Harriett and Sarah, and her mother's illness. Miriam, who begins to feel an intellectual rapport with Mr. Corrie, thinks that she has in him a kindred spirit. In Chapter 3, at a dinner party, Miriam sits across from him, thinks she is able to understand his thoughts, and articulates them to herself. At a later party, however, Mr. Corrie rebukes her publicly; and her belief in finding a kindred spirit is destroyed. Bob Greville visits her and in the course of this visit proposes marriage; Miriam refuses because she cannot accept his idea of the woman's subjugated place in the world. These two relationships bring to the surface Miriam's disdain for men. She becomes increasingly more independent where men are concerned, and she also begins to dwell on the oppositions inherent in the male and female mind. Nonetheless, her earlier attitudes toward men are ambivalent; for, as Joseph Warren Beach has observed, ". . . Miriam in the depths of her nature is very much concerned with the question of a man — someone to take away that sense of loneliness which she both cherishes and shrinks away from."[23]

To take Miriam away from the loneliness is also to take her away from herself. She is not egocentric, but she is conscious of her own destiny and is intent upon finding her place in the world. The adverse experiences with Bob Greville and Mr. Corrie draw her farther away from the world of men; for, since they dramatize the attempt of the male to place the female in an ancillary position in society, she despises the idea of the male-dominated world. Miriam's growing disdain of the masculine mind and its dominance over the feminine sensibilities is compounded by the approaching marriages of Harriett and Sarah. She feels that they will be quickly submerged into the quiet world of domesticity which will never give them freedom to experience the vitality of life: their minds will atrophy and their "curiosities could come to an end." Her last brief period at home toward the end of *Honeycomb* is filled with nostalgia as she recalls times she and her sisters were together. She is acutely aware of the family breakup as her sisters prepare for marriages; one part of her life is over forever. As her mother becomes progressively ill, Miriam is the only one left to care for her; the life of her own which she wants so desperately must wait. Her feelings of independence and her bitter attitude toward men will become the important themes in the later chapters of *Pilgrimage*.

CHAPTER 3

The Dark Wood

I *The Journey Continues*

THE first three chapters of *Pilgrimage* establish in the reader's mind the nature of Miriam's mystical journey. *The Tunnel* and *Interim* represent additional stages in this development, but the mood of these two "chapters" changes as a more serious tone predominates. The theme of a mystical journey to fulfillment and understanding of self continues to be interwoven into the entire fabric of the novel, and the theme is reinforced by allusions to Dante. In *The Tunnel*, for example, there are thirty-three sections just as there are thirty-three cantos in each of the three books of Dante's *Divine Comedy*[1] along with allusions to the "inner circle," "outer circle," and "rim of the world." The Dante parallel reaches its climax in the middle of *Interim* when Miriam attends a Dante lecture and feels the absence of love in her being, in her inability to feel for humanity in universal terms.

The Tunnel and *Interim* were both published in 1919, four years after the appearance of *Pointed Roofs*. *Pointed Roofs*, *Backwater*, and *Honeycomb* deal with Miriam's first three independent experiences as a teacher and later as a governess; but these positions were confined to a narrow world isolated, in the main, from society; and they become for Miriam microcosms which required only fleeting glimpses of the macrocosm outside. As Miriam becomes more exposed to society and enjoys more independence and freedom, her social thinking and philosophical considerations mature. Her surroundings in Hanover, Banbury Park, and Newlands isolated her from many facets of experience because of their relatively cloistered environment. Her wide reading and penetrating insight into experience satisfy her adolescent curiosity, but both

Newlands and Banbury Park frustrate her because of their restrictive worlds. *The Tunnel* and *Interim* tell the story of Miriam's first years in London as she is thrown into the vigorous life of a dynamic city.

When Miriam moves to London and her circle of friends broadens, she is fascinated by the world of ideas which is opened to her; but her greatest sense of fulfillment comes in her feeling of freedom and independence. She takes pleasure in eating alone at a restaurant because it represents to her a carefree life that she has never known. Throughout the earlier chapters, she had scorned the conventional behavior expected of women and had laughed at the many social pretensions of society. Her smoking, her dress, and her religious cynicism are marks of her rebellion against the ordained social pattern for women in the England of the 1890s. But in London she is able to live her own life and to find her fulfillment without conforming to prescribed behavior, and her new sense of freedom is one of the most important themes in *The Tunnel*.

Miriam's early years in London were spent during a time of great social change. As the political historian, Henry Pelling, has written of this period, "The 'New Woman,' claiming the right to an active life, was as much a feature of the period (1885 - 1900) as the new unionism or the new journalism. . . . Both married and unmarried women were prominent in the Socialist movement. . . . Even among the women of the working class the same ferment was at work, though painfully slowly as yet."[2] Against this background with its glimmer of a new freedom for women, Miriam attempts to make a life for herself.

The narrative technique of *Pilgrimage* becomes increasingly more complex as the "chapters" continue because the accumulative effect of Miriam's experience demands it. As she becomes filled with impressions of London, her consciousness relates these perceptions with past impressions which adds complexity to the narrative. The way in which Miriam's consciousness reacts to her early London experience is more subtle, and her mind is now more actively penetrating the meaning of sensory impressions. In the first three parts of *Pilgrimage*, most of Miriam's sensory experiences are merely accepted and enjoyed; but, as her mind becomes more aware of things beyond the senses, her reflections assume an increasingly intellectual character. Because she has difficulty in bringing to her intuitive nature the conceptual powers which add meaning to experience, she is frustrated in her quest for answers to the questions which her philosophical encounters impose.

A result of this probing is a more facile and searching mind but a more demanding one for the reader to follow. Her increasing contact with intellectual groups in London constantly exposes her to new ideas and philosophical positions which she must ponder. Miriam is a part of that group of English men and women who emerged in the last decade of the nineteenth century and "who were anxious above all to develop their knowledge. They were especially interested in social and economic questions. . . ."[3] *The Tunnel* and *Interim* tell the story of Miriam's early years in London, the new people with whom she comes in contact, her first love affair, and the ever-widening focus of her world. Miriam finally feels that she has a life of her own and is participating in the rich current which life affords. The great change that appears in Miriam in *The Tunnel* and *Interim* is that she is no longer a dreamy adolescent locked in her own self-contained world; she has become a young woman striving to find herself in the world at large.

II *The Religious Experience*

In the earlier chapters the reader is aware of Miriam's complex personality and of her groping mind. The Miriam of *The Tunnel* and *Interim*, however, is beginning to formulate her ideas in a world of constantly shifting impressions. Her intuitive faculties, which have always been highly perceptive, are beginning to demand more of her intellect. Determined to be a seeker of truth, Miriam reads, thinks, and constantly ponders the various attitudes toward the world which she encounters in London. No longer in a narrow, confining world, she begins to feel the pulse of life beating within. The reader is impressed with her intellectual integrity. Miriam begins to realize that the power to summon ideas is not the same as the power of the visual memory. Of increasing significance in the novel are her belief and her attitude toward religion. From the first, her reaction to organized religious faith is constantly shifting. She finds the entire structure distasteful and existing in a vacuum. Her religious thinking is of two-fold importance to *Pilgrimage:* first, it reveals her spiritual attitude and awareness of social forms and institutions; second, it shows her increasing desire for intellectual freedom which she feels any formalized religion frustrates. Her spiritual formation is important because she reveals in her opposition to rigid, organized faiths the nature of her own spiritual mysticism which is a major theme of the novel.

Not until later in *Pilgrimage* does Miriam become fixed in her conviction that she must rise above the flux of change and that ultimate reality does not consist in her preoccupation with the moment. From her earlier experiences, she begins to recognize a higher reality in her quest for understanding. Earlier doubts about formal religious belief lead her into a quest for individual spiritual identity which she feels must be found within the self and cannot be provided by any particular sect. Miriam is a spiritual rebel from the beginning, and her rebellion becomes more pronounced in *Backwater* and *Honeycomb*, but it has greater meaning in *The Tunnel* and in *Interim*. As her skepticism moves to agnosticism, her regard for public worship diminishes. While her mind focuses on many theological problems, she often experiences tender compassion for man's loneliness and longings. Her faith emerges as a faith in man; out of her early soul searching, her secular humanism that develops is tied, perhaps paradoxically, to a mystical view of the world. From this fusion of the two natures, her Quaker beliefs later form.

Miriam's later interest in the Quakers is certainly understandable when one recognizes her religious individualism, her mystical view of life, and her moments of illumination. Her agnosticism and her feeling of brotherhood are important elements in her nature. As she broods upon herself, the emotional gravity of the first five "chapters" moves toward a spiritual crisis. Miriam's spiritual development plays an ever increasing role in her journey. The subjective methods of Miss Richardson's art bring dramatic crisis to Miriam's religious quest.

III *Mystical Quest*

Reality postulates systematic unity, but truth sees things in terms of empirical data. Miriam's concern is with truth; therefore, she is preoccupied with the particular and the partial rather than with the whole or the entire. Miriam's quest for independence is clearly related to her agnosticism. In Dostoevsky's *The Possessed*, Kiriloff sees his independence as an attribute of his divinity; and, although Miriam would not be able to articulate this view in earlier parts of *Pilgrimage*, she is moving toward Kiriloff's position. Miss Richardson deals with her character's dilemma as an individual in a world dominated by men, and she dramatizes the conflict Miriam feels between man as an individual and man as a part of the group. Her social feeling becomes intricately interwoven with her spiritual awakening. The recurring religious questions with which she struggles represent Miriam's quest for spiritual understanding, but they also encompass her total being as she attempts to understand her own nature as well as her place in the world.

E. M. Forster has written that the only two possibilities for order in life lie in art and in religion. It is to the exploration of the latter that the young Miriam devotes a great deal of herself. Early in *Pointed Roofs*, one learns of Miriam's attitude toward organized religion; for, when she finds that she will be sharing a room with a French girl, she is immediately relieved that the girl is a Protestant; had she been a Roman Catholic, Miriam felt that she could "not have endured her proximity" (I, 38). Miriam finds out that there are prayers every night at Fraulein Pfaff's school and is "exceedingly uncomfortable." At Bible readings, her interest is in the Fraulein's "slow clear enunciation" rather than in the content: "In spirit she rose and marched out of the room" (I, 49). Later she dismisses a Lutheran sermon as pastoral platitudes, and feels that most sermons are given by men who talk down to captive audiences. As Miriam listens to the sermon with growing resentment, she thinks of Cardinal Newman, who "in the end . . . had gone over to Rome . . . high altars . . . candles . . . incense . . . safety and warmth" (I, 72; ellipses in text).

The background of Miriam's religious skepticism is blurred; however, she has read Charles Darwin and W. E. H. Lecky whose essays dealt with the progress of nature as opposed to theological dogmatism. Her home life was Church of England, but within her family she was allowed considerable religious freedom and speculation. Her father took an interest in her spiritual questioning. The source of Miriam's skepticism seems to be rooted in her wide reading and in her tolerant upbringing in a middle-class, provincial English environment where adherence to a religious faith existed more as a social formality rather than as deep spiritual fervor. The late Victorian culture produced a spirit of independence in social as well as in religious areas; and the young Miriam, subconsciously at least, sees the two as inextricably bound. In *Pointed Roofs*, Miriam is able to look upon religion with the same youthful detachment with which she views social convention; but she lacks the humor in her religious skepticism that she reveals when she debunks conventional social behavior.

A revealing forecast of Miriam's later religious experience occurs in an early scene in *Pointed Roofs* when she visits a Catholic church. The red sanctuary light, shining "like a ruby far ahead in the gloom

. . ." (I, 119), immediately draws her attention and beckons her forward; and this light sets the mood for the scene. After a tour of the church, the priest takes Miriam, Fraulein Pfaff, and Minna to the sacristy in order to show them a jeweled cross. Miriam thinks to herself: "She wanted to stay . . . more than she had ever wanted anything in her life she wanted to stay in this little musty room behind the quiet dim church in this little town" (I, 120). As she walks home, she passes a group of nuns crossing a bridge and asks herself if they are mad. Since religion for Miriam is a highly personal experience, she is edified by the quiet solitude of the little Catholic church; but the sight of a group of nuns in their robes and habits represents to her the formal aspects of the faith which she abhors. When the priest shows her objects, she is able to see meaning in them because of her mystical attachment to things. Miriam's intensely personal and spiritual nature balks at institutional demonstrations such as women in habits and is only concerned with the inner being. The quiet solitude of the mystic offers the only spiritual appeal to Miriam.

As Miriam's abhorrence of "social" religion grows in its intensity, the reader witnesses a rising animosity and a varied play of emotions. Prominent among these emotions come feelings of tension. The critical judgments which she makes toward religious institutions are, however, blurred in *Pointed Roofs*. What begins as cynicism develops into a spiritual crisis in *Backwater*. Darwin's theory, a belief in materialism, and a rationalistic view of the world emerge as positive beliefs in Miriam's consciousness as *Backwater* begins. Similarly, she shows an increasing interest in personal spirituality outside the framework of religious institutions.

In *Backwater*, Miriam's spiritual life takes on more depth as she finds it increasingly more difficult to accept organized religion. Out of her loneliness she searches for spiritual well-being. Her life becomes more private as she takes increasing pleasure in being alone in her room in spite of her feelings of loneliness. She keeps busy by preparing an elaborate toilet and by laying out her clothes meticulously for the next day; but, in these moments between waking and sleeping, her mind runs riot with thoughts and impressions. No matter how orderly she arranges her life, her consciousness keeps her in a constant state of flux. She thinks of two little Quaker girls who wore the same plain clothes everyday, but she feels that doing so would put a damper on holidays were she to assume their drab way of life. The idea of saving money from her meager wages comes to mind, but she dismisses this thought because she has to be one who would "have to give everything up" (I, 271). Deep in her consciousness Miriam believes in a First Cause who brings order to the universe: "There is somebody giving things, whatever goes . . . something . . . left. . . . Somebody seeing that things are not quite unbearable, . . . but the pain, the pain all the time, mysterious black pain . . . (I, 272; ellipses in text). Throughout *Backwater* Miriam is engaged in the dialectic of Christian existence. If she could accept the belief in Christ as God, Miriam would be in accord with Søren Kierkegaard that Christianity is a vital matter of the individual conscience and that it is not a social institution concerned primarily with respectability. Her religious individualism leads her farther away from Christianity because she feels that churches which call themselves Christian see Christianity as merely a comforting and stabilizing element in society and as an ornament in Western civilization.

Earlier in *Backwater,* she is more explicit in her belief in a First Cause: " 'Well, you see, I see things like this. On one side a prime cause with a certain object unknown to me, bringing humanity, all more or less miserable, never having been consulted as to whether they wanted to come to life. . . . But good people with faith, want me to believe that one day God sent a saviour to rescue the world from sin and that the world can never be grateful enough and must become as Christ' " (I, 259). In this conversation with Miss Haddie, Miriam says that "faith seems to me just an abnormal condition of the mind with fanaticism at one end and agnosticism at the other" (I, 259). Organized religion seems to her to be turned outward rather than inward where she can find "the white light in the distance far beyond the noise of the world" (I, 292). Miriam's spiritual consolations come from her mystical moments of illumination, but questions of faith continue to bother her as her religious ideas begin to formulate.

It is in her spiritual development that Miriam recognizes how basically different she is from her sisters and others. She knows that they fail to share her love of quietude, her desire for space, and her love for beautiful things. Miriam, the growing mystic, is at first not so concerned with people as she is with "things"; but from this initial stage she becomes increasingly concerned with human beings. As one critic has pointed out, "For the mystic, however, the experience of things is important."[4] As her mysticism develops, Miriam asks herself: "Reverence for things — had she reverence?" (I, 392). The objects around her have added importance and have meaning far beyond themselves. The furniture in her room, light, gardens, and places constitute part of her total mystical experience; and, at the same time, the ownership of "things" in no way attracts her.

At one point in *Honeycomb* she thinks to herself: "Entrenched in her familiar old dressing-gown, she felt more completely the power of her surroundings. Whatever should happen in this strange house, she had sat for one evening in possession of this room. It was added forever to the other things" (I, 360). Miriam's relationship to "things" is of deep importance to her at this stage of her development because, to her, they are expanded beyond their own reality or place in space; they become for her the most important part of her life before she begins her London years. In *Interim,* after a visit with her sister Eve, Miriam contrasts the importance of people in their respective lives: "All Eve's plans were people. She moved painfully through things, from person to person" (II, 385). This contrast is significant because it reveals Miriam's initial preoccupation with the object rather than with the person; but, as her pilgrimage continues, she becomes more and more involved with human beings; and, as her sense of social justice is awakened, her contact with people increases.

Miriam is not able to formulate at this point a clear philosophy of life, but she is beginning to achieve a comprehension of the world and her relationship to it. Her search for spiritual values carries her inside human experience, and she is beginning to place more faith in her feminine intuition. Her moments of illumination are beginning to become less euphoric. What were once more concentrated reactions to sense impressions are now moments of real understanding. This understanding leads her to believe that man will find divine existence through his own power. In other words, she is coming closer and closer to a mystical view of life.

When mysticism is considered as a theory that knowledge of God or of immediate reality is attainable through use of some human faculty that transcends intellect and does not use ordinary human perception or logical processes, Miriam's difficulty in forming a philosophy that takes in a consideration of man's plight in the world is recognizable. Her awakening social conscience makes her feel at one with her fellow man, but she still feels the need to be alone to contemplate the mysteries of life and to strengthen her spirit. Through her reflections, the reader is able to observe the shifting panorama of events which comprise her external world.

In *Honeycomb,* Miriam enjoys the mystic's quiet solitude in

70 DOROTHY RICHARDSON

nature. In the scenes where she experiences this inner peace, the prevailing imagery of light is always present. She becomes increasingly sensitive to the beauty of the world around her, and her response is more sophisticated. She spends less time enjoying the serenity of places; however, she reads the Bible with more awareness and sees such a great number of diverse ideas there that the power of any single mind to possess them is impossible. The tone of the New Testament sometimes disturbs her: "Some instinct led away from the New Testament. . . . She always sighed regretfully over the gospels and St. Paul, though she asked for them and seemed to think she ought to read them. They were so dreadful; the gospels full of social incidents and reproachfulness" (I, 486). It is to the poetry and the hope of the prophets that Miriam turns again and again. And, too, in the Old Testament, there is not the problem of the God-Man.

Her later reading of Thomas à Kempis' *Imitation of Christ* leads her to contemplate the nature of Christ and His divinity. When she speculates upon the various relationships man feels himself to have with Christ, Miriam ruminates over the fact that Miss Haddie has a terrible fear of God and turned to Christ as a "sort of protecting lover to be flattered and to lean upon" (II, 485). A revealing aspect of Miriam's nature arises as she continues to contemplate the divinity of Christ, for she thinks to herself that she would rather feel Christ than consider a definition of Him. Her mind is still turned to the intuitive rather than to the formal, for feeling Christ rather than defining Him is her existential concept of belief. The theological imagination continually leaves Miriam in a dilemma when she tries to impose formality on her ideas; but, left in an impressionistic, mystical response, Miriam is able to find happiness and consolation. Her despair represents the natural consequence of those excesses of feeling to which she abandons herself rather than the inner turmoil of her mind trying to conceive of Christ's divinity.

The mysteries of Christianity are too complicated for her to establish formally because of the multidimensional reality required; but, more important, she is able to translate divine love into human love which is at the heart of Christianity. For Miriam, the levels of finite and infinite blend when man seeks love in his fellow man. This gradually emerging sensibility is of major significance in *Pilgrimage* because it is indicative of her changing attitude toward the world. She still has valuable moments of solitude; however, she is becoming more and more entrenched in the world and is more involved with the people who come into her life. This involvement with people presents a conflict because it demands more and more from her.

IV   The Tunnel

When *The Tunnel* begins, Miriam's mother is dead; and she has moved to London. Many of her early musings in this part of *Pilgrimage* are about the nature of mortality. She feels that death is the force that robs man of himself. Mrs. Bailey's boardinghouse becomes Miriam's new home, and she has secured a job as a secretary to a group of Wimpole Street dentists. The opening sentence — "Miriam paused with her heavy bag dragging at her arm" (II, 11) — focuses again on the journey motif. As she looks up the stairs leading to her new room, Miriam senses the adventure of the new life that awaits her in London. The stair symbolism still predominates; but, since Miriam's mysticism has turned more toward the world, the stairs tend to suggest reality more than aspects of spirituality, despite the light imagery that still surrounds such ascents. The sense of real things assumes more and more importance; for, as she looks around her new room, she thinks that "You know in advance when you are really following your life. These things are familiar because reality is there" (II, 13). The reflections of light as they play upon the dark room fill her with a sense of expectation: her life in London will last for over a decade.

London is not so thickly woven into the texture of Miss Richardson's fiction as it is in Virginia Woolf's who was endlessly fascinated by the myriad impressions of the city; but London imagery is important to Miriam's moments of illumination because the apprehension of a particular place such as Trafalgar Square often provides her with moments of insight. The impressions of London, the outer world, on Miriam's consciousness, the inner world, is beautifully created by Miss Richardson. Big Ben, Westminster, Hyde Park, and other famous landmarks are encountered by Miriam in her walks through the city, but the less well known areas and places make deeper impressions on her and send her on flights of metaphor. The Londoners who move briskly through the streets provide her with endless fascination: they "were in the secret of London and looked free" (II, 76). The trips through Endsleigh Gardens, where the trees gently wave "their budding branches in bright sunshine" (II, 145); the sound of the bells of St. Pancras; and the houses and gardens along her walks completely absorb her. She is exhilarated by being in the center of beautiful London which she feels is at the hub of life. Each part of London conjures up a different mood, and the city becomes a prairie with a multitude of changing vistas which continually alter thought. Dorothy Richardson shared with Joyce such an accuracy for vivid description that, when writing a description of London while staying in Cornwall, she asked her husband, Alan Odle, to check shop windows in London so that she might record details faithfully.[5]

In the novel, her walks to the Wimpole Street offices where she works are filled with impressions of city life. Although Mr. Hancock is her favorite dentist among the group for whom she works, the daily routine in the office bores her, especially the clerical work which it entails; but she enjoys having tea with Mr. Orley's family who live in the same building. Always curious, Miriam takes home the dental journals to read; and Miss Richardson herself later wrote columns for dental journals. Miriam's attention to details about people and places is noticeably more acute in *The Tunnel* than in the earlier "chapters"; she pays increasingly more attention to the smaller fragments of her impressions such as the type of collar worn by one of the dentists or the distinct sounds of the metal tools they use.

The feeling of being one of London's "working girls" appeals to Miriam and increases her sense of freedom; she enjoys her frugal dinners of hot chocolate and a biscuit at the A.B.C. (a large and inexpensive chain of London restaurants) and the privacy of her sparsely furnished room at Mrs. Bailey's which is all that her salary can provide. Her adverse opinion of men is still in her mind as she begins to think of herself as one of the independent "New Women." Mag and Jan, two working girls whom she meets, acquaint her with some of the joys of being on one's own in London. Their lack of pretension and their unconventional approach to life impress Miriam, and she spends many enjoyable evenings chattering about hair styles, budgets, and the position of the female in a male-dominated world. Some of the carefree subjects that engross Mag and Jan are smoking, cycling, and bobbing their hair — all topics which dominated women's conversation at the turn of the century in England; but their conversations take on a more serious tone later in the novel.

As Miriam's interest in Mr. Hancock grows, her prejudices against men drift below the surface of her consciousness. However, Mr. Hancock, unaware of Miriam's sensitivity, angers her one day when he enters the office and addresses her in an official tone. Miriam immediately becomes disillusioned with him because she thought that, with his interest in Japanese painting and music, he would be different from other men whom she had met. Indeed, his presence in the office had made the work less painful for Miriam ("It was his presence that made me come" [II, 205]). After this incident, Miriam decides for a time that their relationship should remain a business one; but she concludes that "Men are simply paltry and silly — All of them" (II, 206).

The most significant experience for Miriam in *The Tunnel* is her renewed acquaintance with her childhood friend, Alma Wilson; for this relationship becomes a springboard to a new life. Alma is married to Hypo G. Wilson, a writer; and his portrait which is drawn in the later parts of *Pilgrimage* is, as has been noted earlier, a fictionalized portrayal of Miss Richardson's relationship with H. G. Wells. Hypo and Alma introduce Miriam to the literary world of London, and he encourages her to write. At one point, he tells her that "You've had an extraordinary variety of experience; you've got your freedom; you ought to write" (II, 128 - 29); and his suggestions kindle a more intense interest in languages on the part of Miriam.

A later exchange of dialogue with Mag and Jan reveals Miriam's growing interest in writing: " 'Someone kept telling me the other day I ought to write and it suddenly struck me that if any one ought it's you two. Why don't you, Mag?' " (II, 165). When Miriam then asks Jan, she tells her that she does not write for fear that whatever she would do would be mediocre. Miriam is discouraged by Jan's answer because she lacks confidence in her own ability. The confidence and stimulus that she has been looking for is not forthcoming, and her fears of failure return. Miriam's literary ambitions, however, are not to be dispelled. She comes into increasing contact with the literary world and attends Shakespeare's plays, reflects on Lafcadio Hearn's writing, and dwells more and more on the forces of history. The contact with Hypo and Alma becomes more significant in *Revolving Lights* and in *Dawn's Left Hand*.

It is in *The Tunnel* that Eleanor Dear enters the *Pilgrimage*, when Miriam's sister Eve asks her to help Eleanor. Eleanor Dear is a cockney tramp who is completely involved in the struggle for existence; but, unlike Miriam, she has no scruples in planning her survival. Graham Greene describes her kind fully in one sentence: "the lower middle class consumptive clawing her unscrupulous petty acquisitive way through other people's lives."[6] She tries to effect a marriage with her minister and, when this fails, her doctor. Miriam helps Eleanor as best she can in spite of her distaste, and Eleanor finally leaves; but she reappears in later "chapters" of the novel. The contrast between Miriam and Eleanor is a revealing one — it dramatizes Miriam's kindness and good nature in spite of Eleanor Dear's wholly self-seeking approach to life.

On the other hand, Miriam is aware that relationships with others are not always productive; early in *The Tunnel* she thinks:

"Twenty-one and only one room to hold the richly renewed consciousness, and a living to earn, but the self that was with her in the room was the untouched tireless self of her seventeenth year and all the earlier time." "I shall not see them again. . . . I will never again be at the mercy of such women or at all in the places where they are. That means keeping free of all groups. In groups sooner or later one of them appears, dead and sightless and bringing blindness and death . . . although they seem to like brightness and children and the young people they approve of. I run away from them because I must. They kill me." (II, 20)

As Miriam's experiences in London bring her into a wider circle of friends, she thinks of retreating from them:

"And an ill-paid clerkship was its best possible protection; keeping one at a quiet centre, alone in a little room, untouched by human relationships, undisturbed by the necessity of being anything. Nurses and teachers and doctors, and all the people who were doing special things surrounded by people and talk, were not Londoners. Clerks were, unless they lived in suburbs. The people who lived in St. Pancras and Bloomsbury and in Seven Dials and all round Soho and in all the slums and back streets everywhere were. She would be again, soon . . . not a woman . . . a Londoner" (II, 266).

As the world of external reality slowly plays on Miriam's consciousness, she opens herself to the various facets of the world with which she comes in contact. The title of the novel, *The Tunnel*, is appropriately descriptive of Miriam's development since she passes through a period of seeming darkness; but, through this experience she comes out changed — she is surer of herself, she is better able to cope with her self-doubt, and she is more certain of her judgments of people and their motives.

Miriam is still troubled over theological questions in *The Tunnel*. For example, she concludes that Unitarianism clears up "the trouble about Christ" (II, 24) that she evinced in *Honeycomb*. As she explores the tenets of various religious beliefs, Miriam rejects some aspects of one in preference to those of another, but she is not to be held to any one doctrine. When she considers herself in relation to time going on and on through endless space, she cannot accept the idea of eternal punishment because it "makes God a failure and a fool" (II, 93). She feels that one cannot separate God and humanity, and she comes closer to accepting a kind of cosmic pantheism because the sun, the moon, the stars, and the great expanse of sky have a significance beyond themselves. The dual dimension of the Christian kerygma that comes to her mind are the doctrines of Creation and the Incarnation. The doctrine of Creation holds that the world is brought into existence by God from nothing; but Miriam, who has read Thomas Huxley as well as Darwin, is influenced by their view of creative evolution rather than by the traditional theological one. Contrary to the doctrine of the Incarnation, she sees Christ as the ethically fittest Who is killed and will go to heaven. Thinking of her life on earth, she says: "Perhaps this is hell" (II, 95). Like Hulme's "classical imagination," Miriam feels the imagination never forgets that man is involved here on earth and must never cross over the spiritual abyss "up into the eternal gasses" and "go blindly into an atmosphere too rarefied for man to breathe for long."[7] Miriam's attempt to reconcile these two fundamental doctrines in her own mind is still blurred; but this problem of reconciliation, especially in terms of a Christian esthetic, has beset generations of writers. As she moves more and more into literary circles of London, Miriam becomes confronted with ideas which were in the mainstream of English thought at the turn of the century.

The Tunnel reflects the growing facility of Miriam's mind; she is portrayed as able to contemplate more complex relationships as her reading widens and her experience increases. This portrayal is achieved through a subtle juxtaposition of past and present, and by a personalizing of ideas through private reflection. Miss Richardson's stream-of-consciousness technique is applied more adroitly in *The Tunnel*. The interweaving and organizing of complex strands in Miriam's life is handled with increasing deftness to produce an elaborate design. The complex elaboration of time planes is much more successful in *The Tunnel* and in the later parts of *Pilgrimage* because, as Miss Richardson gets closer and closer to her material, the shape of the whole becomes less fragmentary; and life is seen at once in its components and its totality. Miriam's world becomes less landlocked, for the events of external reality as they operate on her consciousness are blended into her mind as her consciousness expands, and this subtle ordering is rendered through Miss Richardson's technique. Miss Richardson is more optimistic than Proust,

76 DOROTHY RICHARDSON

who treats time as a perpetual flow that carries all things away. For her, time is not a hurried aging toward death as it was for Proust who felt Aron must triumph over it; for her, time is a creative flow of all things into a new wholeness.

For example, Miriam's backward glances at her happy days in Germany become a part of her present self: "Today, because I am free I am the same person as I was when I was there, but much stronger and happier because I know it. As long as I can sometimes feel like this nothing has mattered. Life is a chain of happy moments that cannot die" (II, 215). When Miriam reflects on her past in *The Tunnel*, Miss Richardson is at her most poetic: the past is not only part of the present, it is its creator. Miriam's sense of the past is revealed as her thoughts drift into metaphors: "The night was like a moment added to the day; like years going backwards to the beginning; and in the brilliant sunshine the unchanging things began again, perfectly new" (II, 22).

In her mysticism, Miriam still attaches significance to things such as time. Unlike Joyce, Miss Richardson's view of time is not cyclical nor archetypal but more personal and fundamental. Joyce's characters in *Ulysses*, for example, are conscious of abstract or "clock" time; but Miriam is seldom concerned with it except for the composition of place that the toll of the bells of St. Pancras announces. "Real" time or duration, on the other hand, is inseparable from the shifting panorama of life itself. Miriam shares with Joyce's Stephen Dedalus an interest in words and language, even playing on the name "Dedalus" ("I speak tentatively . . . in a dead-alley-Dedal — Dedalus —" [II, 91]), but her sense of time is distinctly different.

The problem of unity in a novel such as *Pilgrimage* is not solved by singleness in point of view nor by restricting the plot to one character's development. Although the narrow focus on the one character magnifies the concept of a journey through life, there must exist, as has been noted earlier, other unifying techniques to bring a sense of order to the amorphous structure of the novel. One narrative technique — along with the symbolic devices and recurring images which have been mentioned such as the stairs, light, and the trunk — is Miriam's reflections on the past. These visions of earlier experiences which the reader has shared with Miriam are seen from a later perspective; and this additional vision enables the reader to see the significance of the event as it plays on her consciousness. But, more important, Miriam's reflections on past experience that took place earlier in the novel tighten the threads and link the parts together. And, as Miriam becomes more mature and her life becomes more self-fulfilling, reflections are not nearly so tiresome.

The title of *The Tunnel* suggests the theme of approaching darkness and uncertainty which surrounds Miriam during her early period in London in spite of her feeling of freedom and her enchantment with the city. Just as every part of the pleasant past adds to the future, so, too, do the dark days cloud the present. She becomes increasingly restless over the problems posed by religion and science as she leans toward a scientific view of life. But she begins to see the inadequacies of a totally scientific view; for, as her social sense is sharpened, she sees that the plight of the human being is unaffected by scientific progress. These emerging attitudes, however, are only ancillary to her growing depression. Her relationship with Mr. Hancock deteriorates because what she thought was a personal interest appeared to be only a professional one on his part along with a common interest in art and lectures. At one point, the Miriam of twenty looks dismally ahead to her life at fifty and sees only loneliness. The last chapters of *The Tunnel* are filled with unrest and discomfort due in part to her precarious financial means, but mostly because of her loneliness and sense of uselessness.

V Interim

Interim is a dull "chapter" in *Pilgrimage;* consequently, it is less able to stand on its own artistic merit than any of the other parts. It lacks dramatic impact because of its presentation; and, although it is linked with the whole, it is static. The title indicates the temporary lack of movement on Miriam's journey, for one outstanding element in *Interim* is Miriam's sense of London. Always alert to her surroundings and absorbed in her own thoughts, Miriam's feelings about the city are beautifully evoked.

As *Interim* opens, Miriam has just arrived for a visit with her friend and former student at the Perenes' school, Grace Broom. Since Miriam is only to spend the Christmas holidays with her friend, a Gladstone bag replaces the Saratoga trunk to reinforce the journey motif. The visit is a happy one for Miriam although because of her awakened social sense, she resents the treatment given to the household servant. But, as the visit continues, she realizes that she and Grace have drawn far apart and that they are no longer able to share the same thoughts or interests. Miriam's conversations with Grace and later with Mrs. Bailey reveal the precision and the craftsmanship required of Miss Richardson's highly restricted point

of view. To maintain the needed balance of thought in order to give
the scene life requires subtle arrangement of thought and adroit
dialogue. The final scene in Chapter 1 between Grace and Miriam
suffers because the reader is interested in the exchange but is unable
to catch its dramatic impact even though the interest is with Miriam.
Miss Richardson fails to balance the scene because she restricts it to
Miriam while leaving Grace inarticulate.

After her visit to the Brooms, Miriam is more convinced that her
life is in London and not in the past. To have tried to remain longer
would have been "making life stop, while reality went on far away"
(II, 320). Reality for her is now London, her room at Mrs. Bailey's
boardinghouse, and even her dull work at the dentists' office. Time
becomes measured by the position of the sun's shadow in her cold
room, punctuated by Big Ben during the day, and tolled in the night
by the bells of St. Pancras.

Miriam is forced by her meager financial condition to live
frugally, but her having bread, butter, and hot cocoa at the A.B.C.
restaurant becomes a special pleasure. When Mrs. Bailey asks
Miriam to give her daughter Sissie lessons in French in exchange for
a meal, she accepts; but she knows that her new privileges as a
boarder "were bought with a heavy price" (II, 336). Her independence has become jealously guarded, and Miriam resents any
restrictions on her newly won freedom.

An important character in *Interim* is a Spanish Jew, Mr. Mendizabal, whose name suggests satanic powers; he offers himself as a
guide to Miriam, and she accompanies him through the streets of
London. A swarthy artist who is far removed from but no less
knowledgeable than Dante's gracious guide, Virgil, Mr. Mendizabal
frequently takes Miriam to a cafe and opens up the world of London
night life to her. She attends a Dante lecture which reawakens her
interest in theology and heightens her speculation about the nature
of love:

Love was actual and practical, moving all the spheres and informing the
mind. That was true. That was the truth about everything. But who could at-
tain to it? Dante knew it because he loved Beatrice. How could humanity
become more loving? How could social life come to be founded on love?
How can I become more loving? I do not know or love any one but myself. It
did not mean being loved. It was not anything to do with marriage. Dante
only *saw* Beatrice. But this is the awful truth; however one may sit as if one
were not condemned, and forget again. This is the difficult thing that *every
one* has to do. Not dogmas. This man believes that there is a God who loves

and demands that man shall be loving. That is what will be asked. That is
the judgment. It is true because it breaks into you and condemns you.
Everything else is distraction and sham. The humble yearning devotion in
the voice reading the lines made it a prayer, the very voice a prayer to a
spirit waiting all round, present in himself, in every one listening, in the very
atmosphere. It was there, to be had. It was like something left far behind one
on a dark road and still there; to be had for the asking, to be had by merely
turning towards it. She looked into the eyes of Dante across the centuries as
into the eyes of a friend. But then these people were the same. It was the
truth about everybody, "the good will in all of us." (II, 355)

As she rides back from the lecture, Miriam is filled with the sense of
love for her fellow man; but she is unable to answer the many
questions that arise in her mind as to what obligation universal love
places on the individual.

Mr. Mendizabal introduces Miriam to Antoine Bowdoin one evening when he comes to play the piano. Bowdoin quickly recognizes
Miriam's appreciation for music and later invites her to attend a party at his flat. She is enchanted with his apartment and says to herself:
"This is Bohemia." The many worlds of London are increasingly unfolding before Miriam and luck brings her new pleasures. These
pleasures of London are temporarily dimmed, however, when she
visits her sister Eve who is an impoverished clerk in a florist's shop.
Although Eve is only taking the job for a short time in order to learn
flower arranging, Miriam is disturbed by her poverty and by her
reduced physical appearance. The sight of Eve working with "wet
feet" upsets Miriam and causes her to renew her contemplation of
the social and economic order. As a result perhaps of her social interests, she reads Ibsen's *Brand* and finds "a sort of lively freshness
all over even the saddest parts, preventing your feeling sorry for the
people" (II, 384).

One important complex emotion which re-emerges in *Interim* is
Miriam's ambivalence regarding men. She is obviously attracted;
but, as can be noted from the description below, Miriam is
simultaneously attracted and repelled:

[There] . . . sat the young Norwegian gentleman, a dark-blue upright form
with a narrow gold bar set aslant in the soft mass of black silk tie bulging
above the uncreased flatness of his length of grey waistcoat. He reared his
head smoothly upright and a smooth metallic glance had slid across her from
large dark clear, easily opened eyes. He was a very young man, about twenty; the leanness of his dart-like perfectly clad form led slenderly up to a lean

distinguished head. Above the wide high pale brow where the bone stared squarely through the skin and was beaten in at the temples, the skull had a snakelike flatness, the polished hair was poor and worn. (II, 328 - 29)

Yet she has admiration about, or even envy of, the masculine out-look: "Men live their childish ignorant lives on a foundation of pain and exhaustion. Down in the fevered life of pain and exhaustion there is a deep certainty. There is no deep certainty in the lives of men" (II, 407). This ability to live above the foundation of pain frees men, nevertheless, from exhaustion and enables them to live produc-tive lives in the world. With thoughts such as these, Miriam is con-tinually contrasting the feminine and masculine points of view — a mental activity which eventually absorbs more and more of her time. Underlying her concentration on this fascinating duality is the necessity for Miriam to project a fully developed feminine point of view.

The feminine consciousness is evoked in any number of ways, most of which are confined to Miriam's musings at the pre-speech level — a level that uses the indirect interior monologue but blends it with other narrative devices. For example,

You were awfully fond of Miss Haddie, weren't you? Miriam peered into space, struggling with a tangle of statements. Her mind leapt from incident to incident, weaving all into a general impression — so strong and clear that it gave a sort of desperation to her painful consciousness that nothing she saw and felt was visible to the three pairs of differently watchful eyes. Poured chaotically out it would sound to them like the ravings of in-sanity. . . . Why would people insist upon talking about things — when nothing can ever be communicated? . . . She felt angrily about in the expec-tant stillness. She could see their minds so clearly; why wouldn't they just look and see hers instead of waiting for some impossible pronounce-ment? . . . I hate you. . . . I have nothing to do with anyone. You shall not group me anywhere. I am everywhere. (II, 306 - 7)

This narrative begins with dialogue, shifts to conventional descrip-tion ("Miriam peered into space . . .") where the third person pro-noun is maintained throughout the indirect interior monologue, un-til, near the end of the passage, Miriam's thoughts rise to the surface of her consciousness and are rendered in the first person. This passage represents a basic pattern within the early "chapters" of *Pilgrimage*, but in the later "chapters" Miss Richardson moves much more freely within and without Miriam's consciousness, and does not exercise careful control. The above passage, however, reveals the increasing dexterity with which Miss Richardson handles the technical and stylistic problems concomitant with her esthetic ambitions which are to create a character whose consciousness is revealed in all of its possible aspects.

Interim is an appropriate title: within *Pilgrimage*, it stands on a plateau that barely advances the narrative, but it contributes to the substructure which prepares the reader for the later "chapters."

CHAPTER 4

The Middle of the Journey

I Deadlock

STRUCTURALLY, if not substantively, *Deadlock* is the most unified part of the thirteen "chapters" of *Pilgrimage*. The relationships of its parts, the thematic function of its ordered episodes, its image patterns, its recurring symbols, and its structural rhythm produce a work of artful integration. An examination of these elements in *Deadlock* suggests the dramatic and the structural principles which Dorothy Richardson fused so adroitly in this important "chapter" of *Pilgrimage*. *Deadlock* contains more elaborate metaphorical patterns and more intricate relationships of those patterns to Miriam's sensibility than any of the previous episodes. A thorough perusal of this chapter demonstrates Miss Richardson's technique and the inclusive harmony for which she strives throughout *Pilgrimage*.

Deadlock is the story of Miriam's love affair with Michael Shatov, the Russian Jew who resides in Mrs. Bailey's boardinghouse. The relationship begins with Miriam tutoring Shatov in English, and it continues with their visits to museums, libraries, and lectures. The subplot deals with Miriam's dissatisfaction with her job and her argument with Mr. Hancock who, at one point, temporarily dismisses her. The major themes of *Pilgrimage* which have been hovering in the mind of Miriam are brought into dramatic focus in *Deadlock*. The themes of woman's basic opposition to man and the liberation of the will achieve dramatic effectiveness although they do not dominate this "chapter." The most significant theme in *Deadlock* is the universal one of loneliness, alienation, and the need for love; and this cosmic theme is revealed through the structure of *Deadlock*.

The major importance of the first scene in terms of the general conception of *Deadlock* is apparent in spite of the seeming trivia of the conversation between Mrs. Bailey, Mr. Gunner, and Miriam, for it sets the movement of the story. The dialogue itself reveals in its cross purposes and fragmentation a basic block between Miriam and the world which surrounds her. In this first scene and throughout the novel, all the social relationships go awry. Between the dull life of the dentists' office on the one hand and her drab life at Mrs. Bailey's on the other, Miriam's life has reached a deadlock — the secluded moments of the past which brought her contentment are gone; but so, too, are the gay conversations heretofore with her sisters and with her friends Jan, Mag, and Mr. Hancock.

Miriam's past eclectic experience of memory and her accompanying sense of joy have vanished, they no longer release the oppressiveness and constriction of time for her and such subsidiary themes of *Pilgrimage* are reduced in *Deadlock*. Persistently Miriam's thoughts revolve around the dominant theme of the self and its relationship with the world — love, alienation, and loneliness are bound together. In the opening scene, Miriam tries, because of loneliness, to restore her friendship with Mrs. Bailey whom she has neglected. When she enters Mrs. Bailey's quarters, she finds Mr. Gunner conversing with the older woman. As their conversation proceeds, Miriam soon realizes that her position as confidante has been usurped by Mr. Gunner and that she has become the outsider. Although Mr. Gunner is a silly bore, he is closer to Mrs. Bailey because he is willing to fill the void of empty hours. As Miriam sits with the two of them, her thoughts quickly turn inward; and she realizes that she is no longer a part of this drab community even with all its boredom and plainness.

Leaving Mrs. Bailey and Mr. Gunner, Miriam returns to the loneliness of her room to view the sky from her window: "Knowing of the sky and even very ignorantly a little of the things that made its effects, gave the most quiet sense of being human; and a sense of other human beings, not as separate disturbing personalities, but as skywatchers . . ." (III, 16). Only during this solitary vigil is she able to feel community with her fellow man — an impersonal association without the disturbance of personalities. Even in the narrow society of the Bailey household, the shape and form of her life had been given focus ("The shapelessness had gone on too long" [III, 15]). Miriam, feeling rebuffed in trying to reenter that community represented by Mrs. Bailey, must seek solace by sharing a small vision of the impersonal sky with unknown members of the human race who, at that moment, share her vision as she gazes at the stars and the expected comet.

This first scene sets the pattern for *Deadlock*. Miriam feels the need to come out of herself to enjoy the "Contemplation of new material" (III, 11) and to enter the world outside herself; but each attempt is thwarted, and ultimately her relationship with Shatov is broken. By the end of *Deadlock*, she is still living inwardly and looking longingly at the world outside that seems to be closed to her. Unlike K in Kafka's *The Castle*, who is willing to accept the community on any values they dictate, Miriam does not accept it on just any terms, nor does she refuse to question its values; she still clings to the integrity of the self and refuses to compromise.

The structural rhythm of *Deadlock* is set in arcs of hope and frustration, and these arcs succeed each other but sometimes overlap. Following the frustration of the first scene, Miriam is buoyed up by the prospect of tutoring the Russian who is arriving at Mrs. Bailey's. Her old feelings of inadequacy return as she contemplates tutoring: "She went down the hall feeling herself young and full of eager strength, sinking with every step deeper and deeper into her early self; back again by Eve's bedside at home, able to control the paroxysms of pain by holding her small head grasped in both hands . . ." (III, 32). When the tutoring begins, however, Miriam regains her confidence and becomes deeply absorbed in discussions with her pupil. Meanwhile, she grows in her dissatisfaction of working for the dentists as her feeling toward Michael Shatov grows. The increasing dislike of her job prepares the readers for the later scene with Mr. Hancock.

Miriam and Michael agree to visit the British Museum together, and she becomes completely absorbed in the prospect. She sees her growing fondness for Michael as symbolic of her fresh beginning. The climbing of the unlighted stairs to her room, which had recently represented the dullness of an ascent to "daily oblivion," assumes a new meaning for her after Shatov's arrival. The staircase to her room is now surrounded with the feeling of "strong, fresh, invisibly founded beginnings" (III, 31). Although the tone of mystical ascent is still present, the sexual symbol of the ascent of the staircase seems to dominate; but such sexual implications are as obviously intuitive as they are throughout *Pilgrimage*. The curious reluctance on the part of Miss Richardson to reveal any of Miriam's physical awakening toward Shatov cannot be taken for a structural flaw, but it raises a serious question about the integrity of an artist who is committed to revealing the entire, complex working of the mind of one individual throughout *Pilgrimage*. The young Miriam should at least express to herself her physical feelings toward the man with whom she is falling in love, and the absence of any concern for physical love, even mentally, by Miriam must stand as a testament to Dorothy Richardson's prudishness — a prudishness which prevents the creation of total reality about the being whom she is trying to represent.

The first development of Section 2 is the growing love Miriam feels toward Shatov, and the second development is Miriam's new feeling toward old places when she views them with the young Russian. Section 2 carries the movement of the novel on an upward arc, for three events in the chapter bring Miriam farther outside herself. In the first, Miriam and Shatov have tea together after their visit to the British Museum — and the familiar surroundings have a new and additional significance for Miriam:

Miriam sat taking in the change in the feeling of a familiar place under the influence of his unconcerned presence. There were the usual strangers strayed in from the galleries, little parties, sitting exposed at the central tables near the door; not quite at home, their eyes still filled with the puzzled preoccupation with which they had wandered and gazed, the relief of their customary conversation held back until they should have paid, out of their weary bewilderment, some tribute of suitable comment; looking about the room, watching in separate uneasiness for material to carry them past the insoluble problem. (III, 63)

In her growing love for Shatov and in her friendship with his fellow Russian, Mr. Rodkin, Miriam begins to perceive the Russian sensibility. Thinking of Mr. Rodkin, she feels that he is "illuminated": "Russians understand silence and are not afraid of it" (III, 67). Miriam's happiness turns inward; her outward feelings reflect the ecstatic state of her mind: "There is no need to go out into the world. Everything is there without anything; the world is added. And always, whatever happens, there is everything to return to. The pattern round her plate was life, alive, everything. . . . What was that idea I used to have?" (III, 67).

A subsequent experience in this "chapter" that reveals Shatov more closely to Miriam occurs when he asks her if she knows of any pawn shop where he can sell something in order to help a Polish friend who is in financial difficulty. Shatov's direct involvement with human concerns nonpluses Miriam for a moment, for she feels that the Pole, although possibly in honest difficulties, is not seriously committed to working hard. Shatov's charitableness leaves a lasting impression upon her, and she regards herself as self-centered because she had planned to join Shatov for supper and did not want anything to spoil the evening. Miriam's realization of her own guilt draws her closer to Shatov because she appreciates him as a man who is truly committed to his fellow man — a man who is willing to extend himself for others.

The third scene of Section 2 reveals Miriam's willingness once again to share her ideas and feelings with someone. She recalls her bicycle accident to Shatov and tells him about Mrs. Bailey's and a Swedish boarder's kindness to her and about the stupid doctor who sewed up her arm with a rusty darning needle which complicated the injury. She tells him about the bill the doctor sent, about her friends who had told her to prosecute him, and about her refusal because "It would not have made him different and I am no better than he is" (III, 82). Miriam astounds Shatov when she relates the fascination she felt at being so near death. As she relates this experience, she delights in the fact that she is able to share her inmost thoughts with another human being; she has at last found herself in communication with another person.

The long third section of *Deadlock* focuses on Miriam's development and on her association with events in the past from the first parts of *Pilgrimage*. When Miriam looks in retrospect at her life, the reader is presented with an excellent view of her development. Miriam's reflections on her past and future unify the entire plot. Now twenty-five, she is a mature young woman who is able to view her past objectively, to look forward to fulfillment, and to analyze her own needs in achieving it.

The structure of *Deadlock* is controlled chiefly by the rhythmic cycle of the seasons and by the patterns of light imagery. *Deadlock* begins in early autumn as Miriam watches a comet soar across the sky. During the late months of the year, Miriam's early fondness for Shatov grows, until, by Christmas, she is reluctant to visit her sisters which once seemed "a goal for which she could hardly wait" (III, 85). Her descriptions of the setting that in the first section of *Deadlock* are drab and colorless become imagistic and poetic. By Section 3, she describes the scene with her old flair for metaphor: "The echoing London sky poured down upon them the light of all the world. Within it her share gleamed dancing, given to her by the

London years, the London life, shining now, far away, in mul-
titudinous detail, the contemplated enviable life of a stranger" (III,
88). Since life begins to dominate the imagery of Miriam's description, light contrasts with the dullness surrounding the earlier
descriptions in the first two sections of *Deadlock*. Light is the chief
pattern of contrast which runs through the story, and it is symbolic of
Miriam's changing mood as her love for Shatov grows.

Miriam's four-day Christmas visit with her sisters establishes the
ultimate separation between herself and familial ties. As the new
year begins, she looks forward to a future that is symbolized by her
anticipation of spring. However, the realization that she is completely and ultimately removed from the world of her past that is
symbolized by the provincial lives of her sisters does not come easily.
The complexity of this realization is revealed in the imagery:

But the interiors of Eve's dark little house and Harriett's bright one slipped
in between her and the pictured town, and the four days' succession of incidents overtook her in disorder, playing themselves out, backwards and
forwards, singly, in clear succession, two or three together, related to each
other by some continuity of mood within herself, pell-mell, swiftly in-
terchanging, each scene in turn claiming the foremost place; moments stood
out dark and overshadowing; the light that flooded the whole strove in vain
to reach these painful peaks. The far-away spring offered a healing repeti-
tion of her visit; but the moments remained immovable. (III, 103)

She returns to London with the knowledge that the Christmas visit
had only been an "interruption," and she joyfully looks forward to a
new life that is to be centered around her feeling for Shatov.

To Miriam's delight, she discovers in herself a remarkable
adeptness, hitherto dormant, at being able to discuss philosophical
ideas with Shatov. Yet she limits herself to formulations of a ten-
tative and experimental nature and hedges on her opinions. Her immediate world, however, has taken on new meaning; and she once
again expresses herself in bright images: "The sky was bright above
the grey wall opposite her window. Soon there would be bright light
on it at five o'clock, daylight remaining to walk home in, then at six,
and she would see once more for another year the light of the sun on
the green of the park. The alley of crocuses would come again, then
daffodils in the grass and the green of the oncoming blue-bells" (III,
104). The anticipation of spring symbolizes her optimism for the
future, but just as the seasonal cycle rises only to fall again, so does

Miriam's love for Shatov. The affair reaches its peak in the heat of
summer, and it ends as the leaves fall from the trees to cover London. The seasons provide, therefore, the structural pattern for
Deadlock, and the imagistic light or dark in which Miriam con-
sistently regards her surroundings is related to her emotional contrasts throughout the novel.

Section 4 is a brief scene with Miriam alone in her room
translating at a little table; for, because of her new happiness, her interest in writing has been resumed. Her room is no longer shrouded
in darkness; and, symboally, the black ink stains which stood out so
before are now "in the warm bright circle of midmorning lamplight,
showing between the scattered papers" (III, 133 - 34). Section 4
carries *Deadlock* on its upward arc as the black moments of her past
(symbolized by the ink spots) are nearly covered and encircled by
the light of the present with its hope for the future.

Miriam's days at the dentists' office with their drudgery now
become a small space that pass in a dream as she looks forward to
Sundays with Shatov. She is able, however, to separate and move
away from the week's work either by attending lectures with Shatov
in the evening or by translating. Even the dull afternoon at work
"could be used in an engrossing forgetfulness of time and place"
(III, 144) as a result of her happiness. But time must move just as her
relationship with Shatov cannot remain one of simple, early love.
Section 5 ends on a note of ambivalence toward the widening arc of
the seasons as time moves into summer: "Time pressed. The year
was widening and lifting too rapidly towards the heights of June
when everything but the green world, fresh gleaming in parks and
squares through the London swelter, sweeping with the tones of spring and summer mingled amongst the changing trees, towards
September, would fade from her grasp and disappear" (III, 144).

As the spring rains wash the London streets and as the world
moves into the cycle of rebirth, Miriam tries to hold the seasonal cycle in her mind — to stop the press of time and to rejoice in a
perpetual spring; but Shatov, the realist, tries to make it painfully
clear to her that she will never be able to withdraw from the cycle of
life that is symbolized by the changing seasons:

"Whatever happens, as long as one lives, there is the spring."
"Do not be too sure of this."
"Of course, if the world suddenly came to an end."
"This appreciation of spring is merely a question of youth."
"You can't be sure."

"On the contrary. Do you imagine for instance that this old woman on the next seat feels the springs as you do?"

Miriam rose, unable to look; wishing she had come alone; or had not spoken. The green vistas moved all about her, dazzling under the height of sky. "I'm perfectly sure I shall always feel the spring; perhaps more and more." She escaped into irrelevant speech, hurrying along so that he should hear incompletely until she had firm hold of some far-off topic; dreading the sound of his voice. (III, 148 - 49)

Sorry that Shatov has become the agent of reality who infringes upon her perpetual dream of spring, Miriam looks upon the gardens and flowers with a determined intensity to perpetuate their growth.

The dialogue above and the subsequent conversation between Miriam and Shatov reveal the characteristic structural pattern of *Deadlock*. The narrative design of the story is defined by the tension between two points of view: Miriam's is the deluding view that she can control her world by bringing to her mind only those things from outside which she chooses; and, ironically, Shatov's view is the ruthlessly revealing one that the forces of the outside world cannot be controlled by the individual. Shatov's view is ironic in that it is through Miriam's relationship with him that she hopefully assumes the ability to control her world. The entire movement of the story is always toward the ironic deflation of Miriam's view. Her false image of a world in perpetual spring inevitably dissolves against the melting force of reality.

The inevitable conflict between Miriam and Shatov grows from their irreconcilable points of view. When the cold logic of Shatov's mind presses in on the uneasy Miriam, she tells him that "race, apart from individuals, is nothing at all" (III, 150). He quickly retorts: "You have introduced here several immense questions. There is the question as to whether a human being isolated from his fellows would retain any human characteristics. Your great [Thomas Henry] Buckle considered this in relation to the problem of heredity. But aside of this, has the race not a soul and an individuality? Greater than that of its single parts?" As Miriam's romantic view of the individual is juxtaposed with the philosophical arguments of Shatov, she clings to her position; as a result, the seeds of their essential conflict have been planted, and they rise eventually to be the enormous barriers that separate them forever. This revealing argument between Miriam and Shatov, their first, takes place in Section 4, which, with Sections 7 and 8, forms the middle part of the thirteen sections of *Deadlock*. After the events of this part transpire, the arc of the story makes its descent to the inevitable failure of their love. The last five sections chart the progressive conflict between the two just as the first dealt with Miriam's growing happiness as her love for Shatov grew.

Miriam attends a series of lectures with Shatov by Dr. J. M. E. McTaggart who proves to her satisfaction that spiritual substance, which is the self, is all that can be said from the metaphysical view to exist. Miriam agrees with McTaggart, but Shatov cautions her to "Beware of solipsism." Ideas and impressions flood Miriam's mind as she plays idea against idea, but she always ends with the supremacy of the individual. As her arguments with Shatov continue after the McTaggart lecture, their discussions develop the contrast between their two points of view. This episode is only one in a series that contrast these two views of the world, for Miriam's interpretation originates in subjectivity, whereas Shatov's "objective" view originates in longer, wider views of the world and its completeness. Since neither person is able to bridge the polarity of vision which exists between them, *Deadlock* continues to unfold as a variation on this essential conflict.

Summer represents the full bloom of romance, and Section 7 opens on this note. The earlier conflicts between Miriam and Shatov have been submerged by their mutual happiness in each other's company; and, although the tension is apparent, their romantic attachment to each other forces their philosophical differences into the background. On "a perfect June morning" Miriam and Shatov are walking through the streets of London when she opens a letter from her employers notifying her that she has been released. When Shatov queries her about it, she tells him of her argument with Mr. Hancock about his unfairness in expecting favors such as ordering books from her as a matter of course. Shatov sympathizes with her position.

The incident with Hancock is significant, for it brings into dramatic focus Miriam's determined individualism and her uncompromising faith in the triumph of the person in society. The same motive which brings about her disagreement with the dentist makes her determined to stay with him: "But I'm not going to be sent away by machinery" (III, 181). Because Miriam resolves to thwart the forces which have temporarily defeated her, she reaches an understanding with the dentist and patches things up temporarily; but her relationship with Mr. Hancock will never be the same, "all possibility of spontaneity between them had been destroyed" (III, 187). This scene not only recalls the beginning of *Deadlock* and Miriam's essential separation from other human beings but also foreshadows her separation from Shatov. The images surrounding her work darken: "The work . . . nothing but the life all around it; the existence of a shadow amidst shadows unaware of their shadowiness" (III, 186; ellipses in text).

When Section 9 opens, Miriam must depend upon "the power of London to obliterate personal affairs . . ." (III, 188). The motif of silence which began in her recognition of Shatov's quiet eyes comes back to Miriam when the entire silent panorama of people who are moving through time ultimately to die sweeps through her mind. From thought of death, she looks backward at her past life; and the possible balance of the past with the future reflects the returning uncertainty of the present. As a result of the change in Miriam, the easy chatter and the pleasant conversation which she had enjoyed with Shatov now turns into testy and challenging dialogue. Her earlier easiness in revealing herself to him is rapidly coming to an end as the events of the novel make their downward arc. Miriam is moving more and more back into herself: "With a parting glance at Mr. Shatov's talked-out indolent vacuity, she plunged, still waiting in the attitude of conversation, into a breathless silence. She would make no more talk" (III, 191).

Still convinced of her need for Shatov, she begins to doubt his need for her; and she finds it difficult now to communicate with him, the liberator of her past and the symbol of her future. The images and symbols of the novel draw grotesquely together as Miriam confronts the prospect of their separation. Just as Joyce used literary methods to symbolize the downward communication path of modern man by shifting the level or style of language from clarity to confusion, Miss Richardson uses dialogue and language as symbols to convey the theme of *Deadlock*. In summary, Miriam starts out to make verbal contact with the outside world, but the fragmented, convoluted conversation with Mrs. Bailey and Mr. Gunner sends her retreating to her room. Her conversation becomes one sided; she retreats into monologue, and soliloquy of unheard and unspoken speech. In the presence of Shatov, however, communication is restored; she begins to translate, to make new words. Life returns; words begin to flow. When Miriam and Shatov attend lectures, the human craving for communication is temporarily satisfied.

But language brings with it the stings of the outside world with its

challenges and its chaos. As *Deadlock* completes its arc, Miriam ultimately rejects communication with all its complications and convolutions. From inside her comes her growing wish for a fertile
silence: "All the things that happen produce friction because they
distract people from the reality they are unconsciously looking for.
That is why there are everywhere torrents of speech. If she had not
read all those old words in the train, and had been silent. Silence is
reality. Life ought to be lived on a basis of silence, where truth
blossoms" (III, 188).

As *Deadlock* nears its end, the patterns of light imagery symbolize
the state of Miriam's soul as she tries desperately to cling to Shatov,
her apparent deliverer from loneliness and alienation. The imagery
reveals the darkening world of inevitable loneliness: "His solid
motionless form, near and equal in the twilight, grew faint, towered
above her, immense and invisible in a swift gathering swirling
darkness bringing him nearer than sight or touch. The edges of
things along the margin of her sight stood for an instant sharply clear
and disappeared leaving her faced only with the swirling darkness
shot now with darting flame" (III, 192). Shatov stands out against
the twilight, but even he cannot brighten "the encircling darkness"
as it "spreads wide about her" (III, 192). Symbolically, however, he
is the torchbearer, the Prometheus who must light the way; for, as
Miriam stands in mystical contemplation of Shatov, his symbolic role
is apparent: "The rosy-hearted core of flame was within him, within
the invisible substance of his breast. Tenderly transforming his in-
tangible expansion to the familiar image of the man who knew her
thoughts she moved to find him and marvel with him" (III, 192).
The dark-eyed Russian Jew stands as Miriam's one desperate link
with humanity, but even he is unable to fight off the powers of
blackness which continually swirl against the light, ultimately
obliterating it.

The light images have become the concrete embodiment of
Miriam's emotional and spiritual turmoil throughout *Deadlock*. Miss
Richardson has elaborated this imagery and fused it so adroitly into
the narrative structure that it reveals her character's nature and
destiny far more powerfully than any of the earlier "chapters" of
Pilgrimage. But, when the images of darkness swirl around Miriam,
she still holds out hope for a future: "The summer lay ahead, un-
altered; the threat of change gone from their intercourse. Tomorrow they would take up life again with a stability; years at their
disposal" (III, 193). The reader, however, is made aware of the in-

herent failure of Miriam's love affair and of her failure with human contact in spite of her glow of hope. The darkness again obliterates any visions of a new life.

Nonetheless, Section 9 opens with an idyllic pastoral note:

> For many days they spent their leisure wandering in the green spaces of London, restored to Miriam with the frail dream-like wonder they had held in her years of solitude, deepened to a perpetual morning brightness. She recalled in the hushed reconciliation of the present, while they saw and thought in unison, breaking their long silences with anecdotes, reliving together all they could remember of childhood, their long exhausting, thought-transforming controversies. And as her thoughts had been, so now, in these same green places, were her memories transformed. (III, 196)

The summer for Shatov and Miriam is a time of peace and reflection. The mood of the season brings them together again, but her thoughts are constantly filled with images of quiet amid the beauty of London gardens. This blissful state is fleeting. As he bids her good night, Shatov asks if she is happy; and Miriam replies, "I think so" (III, 202). As she says this, Miriam suddenly realizes that she should "never tell him more than that" (III, 202). When she leaves Shatov, she chides herself for her inadequate response. But Miriam has begun once again to retreat from communication. She backs away from the world and its concomitant responsibilities to others. Even Shatov's trembling voice attests "to the agonizing powers of his communication" (III, 203). For Miriam, words become "like ghostly hammer-blows upon empty space" (III, 204).

The motif of silence dominates her mind, until the silence and the darkness finally merge into the oblivion that lies before her: "She had taken the first step into the darkness where, alone, she was to wait, in a merciful silence, for ever" (III, 204). The pathos of the novel has neared its completion as the images of darkness and silence gather around Miriam, for her entire psyche is withered by the self-destruction imperative in her nature. Dominated by will, her whole being is in chaos; her body begins to feel restless and numb in the face of her turmoil; and Miriam's psychic unrest is made more poignant by images of circling in the last pages of *Deadlock*. The images of darkness are continually qualified by the word "swirling" to suggest the retreat backward into self. Rather than looking at her life as an upward journey of hope in the symbol of Shatov, she now sees it as a solitary cyclical one that constantly repeats itself with the promise of hope and then despair.

Out of her agony, she feels there must be something behind
"mere statements"; one must look behind the word. The imagery
surrounding her depression takes on cosmic proportions: "The
agony within her must mean that somewhere behind the mere
statements, if she could but get through and discover it, there must
be a revelation that would set the world going again; bring back the
vanquished sunlight. Meanwhile life must pause; humanity must
stay hushed and waiting while she thought" (III, 205). The "vanquished sunlight" and the hushed humanity become the symbols of
her loneliness. Miriam stands as a figure separated from mankind;
she is fearful about entering the world a second time; she is resolved
now to pause and to catch her breath.

The old theme welling up in Miriam — one from earlier
"chapters" in *Pilgrimage* — that comes to the surface is her lack of
faith in men. Men, she feels, are mind and body; and these two
aspects remain separated. Because of their cruel, hard intellects,
"the lovely world of lovely things seen in silence and tranquility . . ." (III, 208) is lost on them. Men, she feels, cannot understand
even the least thing about the worst women. Completely frustrated
at not finding any statement to combat the dominance of the male
will, "she fell [falls] back at last upon wordless repudiation . . ." (III,
209) and retreats "once more to the vanishing securities of her own
untouched imagination" (III, 209). Even Shatov, the most liberated
man she has ever met, is unable to give women the place in the
world that Miriam feels they deserve.

The old black feeling of inequality between men and women
emerges as the active agent that finally destroys Shatov's and
Miriam's love. When a woman collides with Shatov when he and
Miriam are walking, he pronounces a generality about women which
she quickly tests him on. The specific remark itself is deliberately not
revealed in order to concentrate the focus on male prejudice
generally. When Shatov wishes to let the subject drop, she forces the
issue; when he laughs uneasily, Miriam thinks to herself that he is
unaware "that it was a matter of life and death" (III, 214). With all
her pride in womanhood, Miriam questions: "What future could
they have in unacknowledged disagreement over central truth?"
(III, 215). As they walk on through the darkening gray streets of
London, their journey becomes a labyrinth for Miriam. They stop for
tea; and, in the most matter of fact terms, she tells Shatov that there
is nothing more to say because of his low estimate of the status of

woman. When a discussion ensues, the irreconcilable positions of the two become as clear as Miriam's allegiance to womanhood that is not to be broken. But their conversation has a wider range of meaning and a deeper bitterness. Shatov claims to be a feminist, but for Miriam there is to be no discussion. She does not feel there can be any, for the feminine sensibility ranges far beyond what the masculine can perceive. In spite of his openness, Shatov simply cannot overcome his sexist bias.

Deadlock closes with Miriam's visit to Mrs. Bergstein, a gentile who has married a Jew. As Miriam walks through London's West End, the leaves are falling from the trees: "These small green leaves faded and dried and fell crisply, leaving a network of clean twigs to gleam in the rain, and the trellis bright green against the white house-front, suggesting summer all the year around" (III, 223). The seasonal cycle is completed; and the love of Miriam and Shatov which grew in the spring and ripened in the summer inevitably lies dormant and "insoluble" as the story ends with the falling leaves of autumn. And the paradox of Miriam's need and her unyielding resistance to love is captured in the dilemma of the final image of the last two sentences of *Deadlock:* "But alone again with him, the troubled darkness behind her would return with its maddening influence. She was fleeing from it only towards its darkest centre" (III, 229).

II Revolving Lights

As the title *Revolving Lights* suggests, Miriam is in a constant state of flux throughout the "chapter." She continually questions the direction her life is taking on its journey through time and space: "What for? To what end was her life working by some sort of inner arrangement?" (III, 237). Nothing takes on the image of permanence, and her imagination is unable to fix on anything or anyone. Her engagement with Shatov has been broken since the inner turmoil she experienced in *Deadlock;* her tension has subsided somewhat; she is able to look toward the future with ambivalence rather than despair. Miriam and Shatov remain friends; and, when he introduces her to the Lycurgans, a group of socialists, the old conflict between the individual and society rises again, and her interest passes from the socialist movement. She is more content to view man as an individual rather than in the mass. *Revolving Lights* is filled with political and religious philosophy. Miriam is still searching for

the "truth hidden below the surface of life . . ." (III, 396). She
realizes by now, however, that these truths yield themselves up imperceptibly, unpleasantly.

With the discovery that her old acquaintance Eleanor Dear has
become Shatov's mistress, Miriam tries to break away from Shatov
completely. Hypo and Alma Wilson come upon the scene again, and
Miriam becomes increasingly interested in Hypo and this
relationship will develop later. When she spends a month with the
Wilsons in order to rest and forget Shatov, their other guest is
Hypo's mistress; and Miriam becomes jealous of her. Freed from her
relationship with Shatov, she returns to work and her affection for
Mr. Hancock grows. As these changes suggest, the mood pervading
Revolving Lights is one of transition. Miriam is still attached to the
past, but new lights of hope filter in upon her, or, more precisely, as
Gregory has accurately noted: "Subtly the atmosphere of her
friendship with Alma and Hypo began to change its colors, such as
colors in revolving lights change, reblend, and change again."[1]

The shape of Miriam's life has expanded itself beyond the narrow
confines of her work and her dreary boardinghouse existence. Her
mind is now better able to control and render subjective meaning to
outward experience. An excellent example of this process occurs
early in *Revolving Lights* as Miriam comes upon an old woman on a
London street:

The long wide street was now all even light, a fused misty gold, broken close
at hand by the opening of a dark byway. Within it was the figure of an old
woman bent over the gutter. Lamplight fell upon the sheeny slopes of her
shawl and tattered skirt. Familiar. Forgotten. The last, hidden truth of London, spoiling the night. She quickened her steps, gazing. Underneath the
forward-falling crushed old bonnet shone the lower half of a bare scalp . . .
reddish . . . studded with dull, wartlike knobs. . . . Unimaginable horror
quietly there. Revealed. Welcome. The head turned stealthily as she passed
and she met the expected sidelong glance; naked recognition, leering from
the awful face above the outstretched bare arm. It was herself, set in her
path and waiting through all the years. Her beloved hated secret self, known
to this old woman. The street was opening out to a circus. Across its broken
lights moved the forms of people, confidently, in the approved open pattern
of life, and she must go on, uselessly, unrevealed; bearing a semblance that
was nothing but a screen set up, hiding what she was in the depths of her being. (III, 288 - 89; ellipses in text)

In this epiphany, the enormous gulf between objective "semblances"
and subjective "being" is made more clearly manifest to the maturing and more experienced Miriam.

Revolving Lights is a highly concentrated and severely selective section of *Pilgrimage*, for it is built around four distinct yet multifaceted revelations of Miriam's life: fragments of her London social world, her visits with Russian friends Michael and Lintoff, her visit to the Wilson's country house, her return to London and her world there. And, beneath all of these events on the surface level of reality, there lies for Miriam "The truth hidden below the surfaces of life [which was] to yield itself to her slowly, imperceptibly, unpleasurably" (III, 396). The individual's movement through life yields insight and adventure both backward and forward in time, and *Revolving Lights* closes with anticipation as Miriam reads a note from Hypo Wilson: "Dear Miriam — I've headed off that affair. You've pulled me out of it. You really have. When can I see you? Just to talk" (III, 396).

III   The Trap

The opening scene of *The Trap* shows Miriam in the process of finding her new residence in Bloomsbury, but the reader is not told why she has moved from Mrs. Bailey's nor how she met Selina Holland with whom she is to share an apartment. Although in a different setting, this scene of Miriam starting out again is not new to us. With her new prospects, Miriam again hopes for a "world renewed"; but she quickly realizes that neither this drab walk-up apartment nor her new friend offers assurance that her life will be more fruitful. Like the apartment itself, Selina Holland is a drab prototype of Victorian England. Selina, whom Miriam always must call "Miss Holland," is a straight-laced, stuffy, spinster social worker whose ordered and planned existence represents the monotony of life from which Miriam is trying to flee. For one of the most brilliant aspects of *The Trap* is Miriam's penetrating and mature insight into Selina's character. She sees her from so many points of view that the reader has a complete picture of this pathetic human being. Miriam, who contrasts Selina with herself, realizes that, despite all her pathos, Selina is a person who has made a kind of peace with the world through compromise and blindness, something which Miriam is unable to do.

A brooding atmosphere pervades *The Trap*, and Miriam's emotional fatigue becomes more pronounced as the narrative moves forward. In spite of moments of relief such as a party, talks with Densley, who wants to marry her, the reading of a Henry James novel, and the vision of Yeats who lives across the alley, Miriam is unsettled. She despairs because she may never be able to restore the bridges between herself and the world which have been broken. She is now essentially without family or close emotional ties, and her future is as uncertain as it ever was.

The technique of rendering Miriam's consciousness in *The Trap* is handled adroitly. In the earlier "chapters" of *Pilgrimage*, Miriam was revealed directly through the first person only at times of deep introspection and then only for a few paragraphs; but, as Miriam's anxieties and worries increase in *The Trap*, entire sections-of-the novel become stream-of-consciousness ones that are rendered directly in a first-person narration. Unlike Joyce, however, the first-person pronoun is used by Miss Richardson in the interior monologue as it was by Virginia Woolf in *Mrs. Dalloway*.

The one brightness in Miriam's drab, tiny apartment that she shares with Selina is the fact that William Butler Yeats lives directly across the way. His first appearance is a dramatic one, for he appears on the scene like a Grecian god delivered by the rain and thunder:

As the thunder rolled bumping and snarling away across the sky, they saw the figure of a man appear from the darkness beyond the candle and stand pressed close to the window with arms upstretched and laid against the panes. Through the sheets of rain his face was not quite clear. But he was dark and pale and tall and shouting at the storm. So he lived there alone. The storm was a companion. He was alone and aware. Had he seen the new people across the way? A brilliant flash lit up the white face and its frame of heavy hair. The dark eyes were looking straight across.

Yeats: and he lived *here*. Miriam drew back and sat down on the end of her bed. This queer alley was then the place in all London in which to live. He had found it for himself. Was he dismayed at the sight of Philistines invading the retreat where he lived hidden amongst unseeing villagers? She vowed not again to look across when there was any sign of his presence. He should be invaded without knowing it. She would see him go in and out, see without seeing: screening him even from her own observation. And all the time his presence would cast its light upon their frontage. (III, 437 - 38)

Miriam thinks of Yeats throughout her sleepless nights, and she identifies with him. He becomes a symbol not only of her own creative ambitions but of an "appreciator" of the world and of a former of its consciousness. Even this vision, however, is not enough to quell Miriam's inner turmoil; and she must flee the "traps" that bind her to despair. Unable to accept marriage or "free-love," yet incapable of enduring the journey alone in this atmosphere, she must return to the Continent to escape London as well as herself.

CHAPTER 5

The Journey Continues

I Dorothy Richardson and Virginia Woolf

VIRGINIA Woolf was caught in the great dilemma of twentieth-century fiction: she felt as deeply as any other novelists the complexity and fluidity of contemporary life; but, at the same time, she felt strongly the esthetic requirements of art. Although she could never allow herself the freedom of form in the novel that Dorothy Richardson had, she nevertheless valued the bold experiments of Miss Richardson. In February 1919, when she reviewed *The Tunnel* for the *Times Literary Supplement*, Miss Woolf praised the originality of the method and the value of such experiments; however, she still demanded that "Miss Richardson would fashion this new material into something which has the shapeliness of the old accepted forms."[1]   181309

This basic concern for form — the proportion, the symmetry, the strength of order — separates the work of Virginia Woolf and Dorothy Richardson. Although Miss Woolf differed from Dorothy Richardson in her insistence upon "form," she was reluctant to condemn Miss Richardson's departure from that of the established Edwardian novel; and she herself was later to break from the traditional novel. Although the almost tortured concern with form that Virginia Woolf suffered is revealed again and again in *A Writer's Diary*, Dorothy Richardson seems to have made her decision to depart from the established technique of the novel and to never regret having done so despite her diminishing popularity and her great lack of critical attention.

On Monday, 26 January 1920, Virginia Woolf wrote the following in her *Diary*:

Mark on the Wall, K. G. and *Unwritten Novel* taking hands and dancing in unity. What the unity shall be I have yet to discover; the theme is a blank to me; but I see immense possibilities in the form I hit upon more or less by chance two weeks ago. I suppose the danger is the damned egotistical self; which ruins Joyce and Richardson to my mind: is one pliant and rich enough to provide a wall for the book from oneself without its becoming, as in Joyce and Richardson, narrowing and restricting?[2]

At the time she wrote this analysis, Miss Woolf could already have read the first five "chapters" of *Pilgrimage* — *Pointed Roofs, Backwater, Honeycomb, The Tunnel,* and *Interim.* Her reaction to the "form" of Dorothy Richardson's novels is important in viewing Miss Richardson's fiction in the context of the modern novel. That Miss Woolf found the "form" narrow and restricted is not surprising; for, through her own experiment, she was becoming well aware of the problem of the stream-of-consciousness technique in which the thoughts and the feelings of the characters are more important than the action and the dialogue. The novel "without a theme" to which she refers was to be *Jacob's Room,* an obviously experimental work which she wrote in order to find her "form" for *Mrs. Dalloway* and *To the Lighthouse.*

However, to estimate what, if anything, Virginia Woolf learned from Dorothy Richardson is difficult; but, at the same time, it would be too simple to say merely that Virginia Woolf profited from reading Miss Richardson by recognizing the weaknesses in the early "chapters" of *Pilgrimage.*

Miss Woolf later changed her opinion of Joyce; but more importantly she became convinced, despite her earlier strictures on Joyce and Miss Richardson, that this new "form" liberated the novel from those readers who insisted on plot and love interest.[3] As she experimented with the stream-of-consciousness technique and realized its possibilities, she was able to perfect it and to render it into meaningful art. The problem with Miss Richardson's fiction, as Miss Woolf saw it, was that the self — the "center of consciousness" — had seemingly run away with the control of the novel. The sustained inside view of Miriam Henderson that Miss Richardson presents the reader certainly gives him a vivid picture of her mind; but this same closed structure with its constant reliance on the one character, however great her sensibility, weakens the force of the early "chapters" of *Pilgrimage.* Moreover, the reader is in danger of receiving the impression that it is all Miriam's world and that there is no world outside. In other words, the very privacy of the narrator tends to limit the life that Miss Richardson is attempting to create.

The world becomes Miriam, and the reader is permanently forced to see it through Miriam's mystic rhapsodies or frustrations. When she awaited the reviews of *Jacob's Room,* Miss Woolf expressed a similar fear: "Now what will they say about *Jacob?* Mad, I suppose: a disconnected rhapsody; I don't know."[4]

Miss Woolf saw the need for unity within the "form," and it was in *Mrs. Dalloway* that she developed her stream-of-consciousness technique.[5] The novelist who adopts the stream of consciousness is faced with the problem of giving some kind of unity to the free associations of the characters' minds in a work of fiction. One example from *Mrs. Dalloway* should point out an important device used by Miss Woolf to give unity to time and place. The chimes of Big Ben, the skywriting, and the gray limousine are devices which link the various characters to the outside world and to one another although they never meet. The way in which each of the characters reacts, whether it be Septimus Warren Smith or Mrs. Dalloway, to outside phenomena reveals their natures but at the same time establishes the essential unity in the novel, namely, of place and time; yet, it is not clock time that is important, but the character's reaction to the world. Readers are aware of the outside world in *Pilgrimage* although it is permanently rendered in the psyche of an individual.

It also seems that Virginia Woolf shifted more freely and adroitly between the planes of action and pure memory than did Miss Richardson. It was perhaps Virginia Woolf's dissatisfaction with the early "chapters" of *Pilgrimage* because of their narrowness and their preoccupation with the "egotistical self" that led Miss Woolf to search for a more flexible method to show that life "is not a series of gig lamps symmetrically arranged . . ." but rather "a luminous halo, a semi-transparent envelope surrounding us from the beginning of consciousness to the end."[6] Before one praises Miss Woolf too highly, however, one must recognize, as Robert Humphrey has indicated, that all stream-of-consciousness fiction is not alike and that there are nearly as many different ways of rendering it as there are novelists using the technique.

Miss Richardson's technique relies most heavily on imagery (which was discussed at length in Chapter 2) and it is in the image that she is able to render her character:

[Miss Richardson] . . . for the most part simply describes the impressions which Miriam encounters and states the associations which Miriam has with these initial impressions. This is done usually in terms of imagery, not

narrative. It is concrete, not abstract; and it is reflective, not dramatic.
Dorothy Richardson handles this approach so skillfully that the reader comes
to identify images with certain moods of the character, and he comes to be
able to fill in the blank spaces in Miriam's own private psyche.[7]

The use of this technique obviously makes for a great deal more expansion of the novel (hence the great length of *Pilgrimage*), but
Professor Humphrey's observation is extremely acute. As the reader
becomes thoroughly accustomed to the pervading images of light
throughout the novel, he is able to fill in the "blank spaces" of
Miriam's psyche; she begins to be understood and real in a way no
other character of fiction is. The reader is, as totally as possible,
"within her mind." The problem of sustaining interest diminishes as
the reader accompanies Miriam through her world. As one reads
Pilgrimage, one is in a world where everything flows from the same
source — Miriam's life and the universe in an uncanny way become
one. A nearly absolute sense of continuity is established between
Miriam's consciousness and the worlds of time, nature, and the self.
But from this very continuity there is also the clear vision of dishar-
mony and individual isolation between the movement of the world
and the self, or perhaps it is that same feeling that Georges Poulet expresses when writing of Maurice De Guerin: "The feeling of a
monstrous acceleration of movement by which the world and the self
find themselves swept along."[8] In the later "chapters" of *Pilgrimage*, the reader is able to make with Miriam the synthesis of present
and past private symbols. This function of memory with image
would explain why Miss Richardson insisted on the collective title
Pilgrimage and preferred to call each new title only a "chapter" of
the long work even though one could read each as a self-contained
novel.

   To understand this technique, however, does not remove the
charge of diminishing returns. The question asked about *Finnegans
Wake* applies equally to *Pilgrimage* — how much is the author per-
mitted to demand from the reader? The answer certainly lies in the
esthetic satisfaction of the reader, and Miss Richardson never
wavered in the integrity of her commitment to her artistic ideal;
throughout her life, in spite of the relative public and critical failure
of *Pilgrimage*, she retained a faith in her work. However, her
technique did not remain static, for she developed its precision. In
fact, the last five completed "chapters" of the novel reflect a significant development in her art. Indeed, each of the five remaining
chapters, as well as the unfinished *March Moonlight*, gives us an ad-

ditional example of her growth and technical artistry. Although individual earlier "chapters" are brilliant in many scenes, Miss Richardson is able to sustain a high quality throughout the last "chapters."

Apart from technique, it should be pointed out that although Virginia Woolf's art surpasses Dorothy Richardson's in its intensity and poetic concentration, Miss Richardson's offers far more range in subject matter in spite of the narrow focus on Miriam Henderson. Unlike Miss Woolf, the author of *Pilgrimage* deals with people from nearly all social strata.

In *Pilgrimage* there are shop girls, dentists, writers, immigrants, school teachers, and people from many other walks of life. Miss Richardson's characters range far beyond the confining environment of Virginia Woolf's Bloomsbury and *Pilgrimage* provides a broad range of profiles as well as dimensional characters from various facets of English life during the years covered in Miss Richardson's "chapters."

II Oberland

The last words of *The Trap* are "Away. Away," and they establish the distance between Miriam and the close and narrow world of her London as she leaves for a long stay in Switzerland. As Horace Gregory has pointed out, "What Switzerland brought to Dorothy-Miriam was a renewed sense of her own Englishness; and with that, the feeling of being a spectator, the awareness of seeing other people's lives (her fellow guests at an Alpine resort) with the eye of a novelist."[9] Some of Miriam's most acute observations in *Oberland* center on a little girl, Daphne, who is abjectly lonely. The portrait of this young girl is a remarkably fine and insightful study of the lonely world of a child; and, as the novel explores this world, Miriam comes outside herself and rebuilds her own private habitation. The mountains are an ideal place.

Despondent, near despair as *The Trap* ends, Miriam embarks for Switzerland in an attempt to recover her equilibrium. The mountains, the air, the wildness, and the calmness of nature restore in her the assurance that life still has meaning. Buoyed up by the beauties around her, Miriam frequently describes her surroundings in a lyrical reverie. Her mystical nature, which had been partially obliterated by her failures in human contacts in London, is attuned to the splendor of the natural surroundings of Switzerland where she feels a transcendence from earth. T. S. Eliot's line from *The Waste*

Land, "In the mountains, there you feel free," echoes throughout *Oberland.*

Her entanglements of London — Michael Shatov, Mr. Densley, Hypo Wilson, and Miss Holland — temporarily fade from Miriam's mind during this brief, lyrical interlude. Her social, theological, and philosophical ponderings subside as she becomes temporarily liberated from her everyday existence and even from her caustic view of men. Although *Oberland* portrays Miriam as being temporarily halted on her journey, the mystical nature of Miriam's "pilgrimage" is reinforced by this brief hiatus. She takes in the immediate experience of meeting new people in a new setting; and, although she is extremely perceptive in her observations about them, they remain largely detached from any integration into her immediate life. In this "chapter" Miriam enjoys, therefore, the romantic's escape from the world, however incomplete. Reason and reasoning, the troubled thoughts of everyday reality are transcended; but all immediate awareness is taken into Miriam's dreamlike consciousness. She writes her friends in London, especially Densley "of the warm heart and wooden head," but from the distance they seem "rearranged."

The passages describing the mountain scenes in *Oberland* contain some of the most beautiful and powerful lyric passages in *Pilgrimage.* Miss Richardson is not only able to evoke the beauty of the Swiss scene but also to show clearly the effect of the setting on Miriam. As Miss Richardson takes her character farther and farther on her mystical quest of life, her art in providing an active and revealing setting increases. Just as the old room at Mrs. Bailey's and the dismal apartment shared with Miss Holland reflect the dullness and near despair of Miriam's life, the setting in *Oberland* signifies the possibilities of freedom, fulfillment, and inner peace. The setting of *Oberland,* with its gorgeous scenes of natural beauty, contrasts sharply with the ugly little apartment in Bloomsbury from which Miriam has fled. In her mystical quest, Miriam is trying to transcend time and space; therefore, Miss Richardson must fulfill the difficult task of creating a setting which provides her character with an opportunity to "raise herself" from past and present; and Miss Richardson succeeds in *Oberland.*

III   John Austen and the Inseparables

During the three-year interval between the publication of *Oberland* (1928) and of *Dawn's Left Hand* (1931), Miss Richardson wrote a brief critical study of the wood-cut artist and book-illustrator John Austen, entitled *John Austen and the Inseparables* (1930). In her study, she makes several interesting observations about the interrelationship of the visual arts to literature; and one of these is especially noteworthy:

> For whereas the artist comes to his medium from afar and consciously lives through his early struggles therewith, the writer, whatever his struggles, is handling a medium he has used from infancy onwards and whose arduous acquisition and final mastery he has long since forgotten. It lies, ready for use, stored up within him in fragments each of which is a living unit complete in form and significance. Within this medium the reader is also at home.[10]

The literary artist uses words, and words are not only common to him but to his audience since both have been using them since infancy. With the visual artist, however, the beholder is not nearly so aware of the medium or the "esthetic approach" which takes the work of art toward "the idea of significant form."[11] The viewer of a cathedral or statue, in other words, is not so familiar with the artist's techniques as he is with the literary work. According to Miss Richardson, this close relationship between literary artist and reader makes literature "humanity's intimate." Unlike a creation of the visual arts, a "book yields its treasure not directly in a single eyeful, but extended in the course of a prolonged collaboration between reader and writer . . ."[12]

This "collaboration" on the part of reader and author is precisely what is required in *Pilgrimage*. "All literature," continues Miss Richardson "is to some degree pictorial."[13] It is through the imagery of *Pilgrimage* that Miriam's psychic being is rendered. As the novel progresses, the imagery begins not only to function as revelatory of Miriam's mind but to describe scene, create mood, and blend the temporal and the spatial, the abstract and the concrete. It was perhaps her growing awareness of the visual arts that brought Miss Richardson's imagery in the later chapters of *Pilgrimage* into sharper focus. The lines become cleaner as Miriam perceives the world around her as a mature adult. More important, as will soon be seen, the imagery in the later "chapters" not only brings a fuller meaning to Miriam's world but is interwoven into the fabric of the novel in such a way as to contribute to the richer texture and growing density of the book.

IV   Dawn's Left Hand — *The Maturing Technique*

Dawn's Left Hand provides an excellent opportunity to look at the maturing technique and method in *Pilgrimage*. By the time the reader has reached this tenth nearly self-contained "chapter," he is clearly aware that Miss Richardson is less concerned with Miriam's experiences than she is with the experiencing mind as it relates to the events, people, and places it encounters and takes into its sensibility. Shatov, Hypo Wilson, if not Miss Holland, and Mr. Densley are round characters in E. M. Forster's terms; but they have only been important to the reader insofar as they are related to Miriam, for the reader never views Hypo talking alone to his wife Alma, nor Shatov attending one of his socialist meetings. Their outside experiences are known by the reader only if they are related to Miriam and have affected her sensibilities. Furthermore, equal importance is given to almost all events and situations whether Miriam is changing the furniture in her room or having her last meeting with Shatov. This fact, of course, raises the issue of "esthetic distance." But, for the mystic, the seemingly unimportant and valueless become paramount.

Miriam's return to London brings her once more into close social contacts, but people themselves can also offer an escape into herself: "she was glad to be escaping back into the company of people who moved mostly along the surface levels and left her to herself" (IV, 192). This preoccupation with private sensory awareness tends to restrict Miriam's thoughts to seemingly trivial matters and results in sensory boredom; colors, shapes, reflections, proportions, lines, and shades merge within what comes dangerously close to being mere static enclosure without refinement or definition. These images are relieved — if just barely — by the subtle arrangement of reactions by Miriam to this phantasmagoria of images which are apprehended by her senses. Central to an understanding of these minute descriptions of nearly every detail encountered by Miriam's senses is the way in which they blend to form heightened impressions in Miriam's mind which evoke feelings of freedom for thought as well as for a unique awareness of time.

These times of flooding sensory impressions, often continuing for several pages, evoke the "depth of inner being" which is so important to Miriam's own self-revelation, self-identity, or self-discovery; and the contribution to one or the other depends upon the particular experience itself. Miss Richardson's artistry, however, does not lie in the evocation of the images as they blend and merge in Miriam's mind — on the contrary, they often cause sensory boredom on the part of the reader; instead, her artistry lies in the way in which she uses such material to plumb the depths of Miriam's own being and explore the deepest reaches of her person — and this exploration redeems the entire purpose and technique.

Miss Richardson's insistence upon the single human being has, however, obliterated her as the narrator. Like Henry James in his later fiction, Miss Richardson has created a "central intelligence" in *Pilgrimage;* however, unlike James, she is not able to bring this technique to its full fruition. For James' "central intelligence" technique enabled him to bring together effectively both the dramatic and the narrative. In the early "chapters" of *Pilgrimage,* Miss Richardson, except in a few scenes, lacks James' virtuosity and is unable to deal fully with Miriam's experiences in dramatic terms. When Miriam is in a group, the reader is unable to get the total effect of mood, tone, or nuance. As *Pilgrimage* grows, however, the esthetic design for which Miss Richardson is continually striving is realized; and two examples of her success can be illustrated from *Dawn's Left Hand.*

This "chapter" deals with Miriam's return from her fortnight's stay in Switzerland which was for her a "golden period" within her life: "Piecemeal, everything piecemeal. What Oberland had been, apart from people, no one would ever know. Yet its beauty had entered into her for ever; its golden glow must surely somehow reveal itself. It lay even over the nauseating, forgotten detail of Flaxman's now rapidly approaching" (IV, 140). Since she has returned to London, she must face the same problems from which she has retreated; but she faces them while still basking in the glow of her mountain retreat. She rejects Mr. Densley's proposal of marriage and the comfortable Victorian life which he represents. Amabel, a young French girl, becomes very close to her. By now Miriam has left the drab quarters she shared with Selina Holland and has returned to Mrs. Bailey's boardinghouse. After a great deal of soul searching, she consents to becoming Hypo Wilson's mistress; but she finds him a pathetic sex partner and gives him up by the end of *Dawn's Left Hand.* In the meantime, her employer, Mr. Hancock, has married; and her job seems to her all the more meaningless.

These are the circumstances of *Dawn's Left Hand,* and two scenes illustrate Miss Richardson's growing power.

The structure of *Dawn's Left Hand* is built around Miriam's continuous search for self-identity, and this search involves freeing herself from two ties with the opposite sex, counterbalanced by a growing friendship for her young friend Amabel. The two scenes — the first in Section 3 where she rejects Densley's proposal of marriage and the second in Section 4 where she refuses to carry on her liaison with Hypo Wilson — are crucial in this "chapter". Miriam's decision about rejecting both Densley and Wilson is a much more deeply felt and revealing one than she made about Michael Shatov which was emotionally reserved in order to preserve her own independence.

The scene with Densley is a masterpiece of clear-cut portraiture. Densley is the prototype of the late-Victorian male who, despite his kindness, continually belittles the intellectual ambitions of women. Although Miriam realizes that a marriage to Densley would bring her comfort and respectability, she knows that it would rob her of any freedom to think and act as her emotions dictate. In this scene, the character of Densley is adroitly revealed through Miriam with a minimum of dialogue. Densley's cautious humanitarian impulse, his aristocratic bearing, his sense of order and proportion are a mixture of constant wonder and amusement to Miriam. She sees him, in spite of what she considers his backward social values, as a kind and generous figure.

Upon her return from Oberland, Miriam is "summoned" by a note to visit Densley at his office during her lunch hour. Before she enters, Miriam is preoccupied with doubts and questions, since she is not certain about what to expect. She remembers that her letter to him from Oberland was perhaps so effusive that it might have led him to think that she was more attached to him than she had intended. When the maid lets her into Densley's study, which is also a part of his medical office, he is "standing there in silhouette against the long window-blind yellowed by the sunlight it was keeping out" (IV, 144). From the first, light plays an important function in the scene; it is through the light images that the significance of the encounter reveals itself to Miriam. Flustered and puzzled, Miriam flounders in the semi-darkness; the drawn shade is associated with sickness, and her mind flashes back to her first meeting with Densley who was brought by Eleanor Dear to her sickbed.

After a brief greeting Miriam notices with a cruel irony of which she is not immediately aware, a rose bud in Densley's lapel and asks him if he has attended a wedding. For her, the rose bud is an outward sign of Densley's proper Victorian manner. She recalls this same rose bud after she leaves Densley's office and is reminded of their essential incompatability: her sense of freedom as opposed to his concept of a wife, his belief that he knows her mind, and his utterly practical life that contrasts with her mystical sense of being.

Throughout the scene Miriam, searching for meaning in gesture and tone, tries to interpret Densley's actions. Readers are not so totally absorbed in Miriam's thoughts that they fail to see the forced calm of Densley as he tries to broach the subject of marriage. The scene is totally revealed through Miriam, but the dialogue with its penetrating incisiveness portrays Densley's groping under a calm and a rather detached facade that enables the reader to appreciate the full dramatic quality of the scene which is not diminished by the restricted point of view as it often is in early "chapters." Because the tension of the scene is fully and powerfully rendered by Miss Richardson, the reader realizes Densley's plight more than Miriam does; and, because of this fact, he is all the more conscious of her thoughts as she tries to interpret Densley's actions and words.

When he finally proposes marriage to her indirectly, Miriam is unable to speak. Mistaking her ambivalent silence for outright rejection, Densley makes a few inane comments before Miriam leaves; and he preserves his ego in a typical Victorian manner.

As she walks down the little London back street after leaving Densley's office, Miriam thinks of the life from which she has escaped:

she turned again towards that strange moment trying to recall the experience. But it was the visible pageant of marriage that rose before her eyes; so suitably, she felt now, a floral pageant. Wistfully, . . . she watched the form of the satin-clad bride adream in a vast loneliness of time that was moving with the swiftness of the retreating movement of the years that were leaving her for ever. . . . saw the led bride, . . . measuring off the last moments of her singleness, reluctantly until the other equally lonely representative came in sight, waiting for her at the altar. . . .

She heard the two voices sound out from time into eternity, amidst a stillness of flowers. . . .

It was because life with Densley would hold the light of an in-pouring eternity that she had found herself willing to throw in her lot with his. In Hypo there was no sense of eternity; nor in Michael. . . .

Vibrating within her . . . was relief. And as she surveyed the little back street, where now she found herself, in search of food . . . she felt, . . . the decisive hour that had just gone by slide into its place in the past. . . . (IV, 154 - 55)

Miriam, filled with both resentment and relief at this passing spectacle of marriage, then thinks of the "journey" before her and her mind quickly turns to her mounting hunger, because she has missed her lunch. Miriam is back again in the mainstream of London looking for a tea shop when she has only ten minutes to do so before she has to return to work.

This scene reveals the growing control Miss Richardson exerts over her material: her imagery is more mature and subtly integrated into the narrative. The play of light in this scene with Densley is unobtrusive, but it shows Miriam's shifting attitude toward Densley and the life which he represents to her. The style is more deliberate as it conveys a subtle analysis of character rather than merely recording the maturing imagination of Miriam found in earlier "chapters." Throughout the scene Miss Richardson is able to sustain the dramatic elements without overtreating Miriam's perceptions and to maintain, therefore, the balance needed to bring the scene to life. In other words, the reader must see Densley through Miriam; but, at the same time, he reveals himself through the dramatic and psychological situation created by the narrative.

The hotel scene with Hypo Wilson in Section 9 is the climax of *Dawn's Left Hand,* and Miss Richardson brilliantly renders Miriam's complex human emotions and sets them against a careful portrayal of Hypo Wilson's biological needs and human drives. The universal ramifications of this encounter are vividly realized, for the eternal conflict between man and woman comes clearly to light through Miriam's deep probing of her relationship with Hypo. Furthermore, the reader notes from the beginning of the long chapter that Miriam is coolly detached in spite of her involvement with Hypo; and, because of her self-control, she is able to view the affair with Hypo with far more objectivity than she evinced with Michael Shatov. Her sense of distance and her clear insight into male and female natures give this scene its significance.

Early in the evening before Hypo and Miriam engage in sexual relations, Miriam is clearly aware that her inner being is far removed from her immediate involvement with Hypo:

Far away from him and from her surroundings her spirit seemed to flee, demanding peace, and to-night, at no matter what cost in apparent idiocy or ill-humour, she would reach that central peace; go farther and farther into the heart of her being and be there, as if alone, tranquilly, until fully possessed by that something within her that was more than herself. If not, if she remained outside it, if he succeeded in making her pretend, though he never knew she was pretending, to be an inhabitant of his world, then again they would squabble and part. (IV, 219)

The tone throughout the whole scene remains objective and detached. Miriam is simultaneously enchanted and repelled as she contemplates the nature of man as she sees it in the brilliant but pathetic Hypo Wilson. Indeed, he becomes for her the generic man with all his frailties and strengths.

Miss Richardson's narrative technique increases the penetrating insight into the significance of the scene when, before Hypo and Miriam sit down to the table spread before them, Miriam gazes into the mirror: "Gazing into the depths of the mirror's fly-blown damp-mottled reflection of a dark curtain screening a door in the opposite wall, she was aware of herself there in the picture, lit from behind, obstructing the light that presently again would lie across the mirror when she turned to join the party: him, and herself representing to him a set of memories amongst other sets of memories" (IV, 219). This incident recalls a similar one in Joyce's "The Dead" in which Gabriel Conroy looks into the mirror prior to the crushing blow to his ego when he finds out about his wife's dead lover. Miss Richardson uses this same naturalistic detail with equal success, for this visible moment for Miriam has an impact on the remaining action of the scene. Not a symbol of narcissism, the mirror functions here as a sign of objective reality; for Miriam clearly sees herself and what her relationship to Hypo is from his point of view as well as hers. The image of light is also suggestive; it foreshadows her ultimate rejection of Hypo as a lover because she sees that her immediate actions are blocking out the light that is necessary for her to find her destiny.

Regardless of Miriam's liberation from the suppressive Victorian moral standards, she is drawn to consider her past in much the same way as Joyce's Stephen Dedalus. Her sister Eve represents the respectability and the old values of her earlier life which she has rejected. In Miriam's present life she is "surrounded by people all of whom Eve would see as 'living in sin' " (IV, 230). Although she does not know her fate, she is able to come to terms with her life without the old frustrations. Her life is moving, "not back into the past, but forward, it seemed, into a future that belonged to it and drew her to itself, to where by nature she belonged" (IV, 230). The theme of the errant child who breaks from the values and surroundings of his parentage was prominent in British fiction and can be seen in George Meredith, in Samuel Butler, later in Joyce's *A Portrait*, and in Virginia Woolf's *Jacob's Room*. The feminine counterpart of this conflict between generations is rendered in Miriam's search throughout *Pilgrimage* and is never far below the surface.

Later in the scene, Miriam remarks to Hypo that she has heard of

Arnold Bennett but has not read his *Clayhanger;* and Hypo tells her
that Bennett is a Realist and that she would like him. *Clayhanger* is a
novel that would have poignant relevance for Miriam because it is a
story of a young man in bitter conflict with his father. The setting of
the novel is typically Bennett's: the drab industrial provincial
background of Northern England. The allusion to Bennett's novel
forces the reader to recall not only the large structure of *Pilgrimage*
but also Miriam's immediate conflicts: she is a product of an older
generation as well as of the present one. The allusion to *Clayhanger*
is also tightened by Hypo's reference to the drab life which Miriam
leads and to her "borderline" poverty.

In *Backwater* and *Honeycomb* the material of the dramatic present was often lacking in intensity and in narrative quality because
the reader was forced to shift from the scene at hand to Miriam's experiencing of the event through her psyche. But, as the reader may
see in the above episode with Hypo Wilson, Miss Richardson has so
perfected her technique that she presents a finely wrought picture of
the external forces (to which Miriam reacts) and the inner self (as she
experiences such forces) by blending both into the movement of the
narrative.

At the end of *Dawn's Left Hand*, Miriam's journey has become no
less easy, for her temperament still rasps at the social environment
surrounding her. Miriam knows that she will never be able to live by
a set code of values nor by any social or religious doctrine. Despite
such knowledge, she retains her inherent sense of futility, struggle,
and uncertainty. It is in her struggle with these problems that she
justifies her quest for a richer life. Nevertheless, Miriam is haunted
by a feeling which echoes one in Goethe's *Wilhelm Meister:* "While
you are making the choice of life, you neglect to live."

V   Clear Horizon

The title *Clear Horizon* suggests Miriam's mood at the close of
this "chapter" when she has broken all her previous ties in London
and starts afresh on her journey, that in *Dawn's Left Hand* ended on
a note of gay freedom. Having severed relations with both Densley
and Hypo, Miriam felt liberated; and London again instilled happiness as she traversed its streets. Her friendship with Amabel had
restored her "feminine spirit," and she felt she had transcended the
need for the world of men and no longer needed to compete; by ex-
cluding them from her world, she need not suffer from their lack of
sensibility. Her flight into fantasy is short lived, however, as the

events in *Clear Horizon* reveal themselves; for each circumstance in *Clear Horizon* sinks Miriam farther and farther into depression. At first, Miriam is happy about the possibility that she may be pregnant, but she discovers that she is not. Amabel has fallen in love with Michael Shatov. When Amabel is arrested during a demonstration by the Lycurgans and tries to make first-rate melodrama out of it, Miriam is upset over Amabel's childish reactions.

One of the most revealing elements within this "chapter" is the contrast between Amabel and Miriam. In spite of Miriam's clear rejection of middle-class values and conventions, she can never become an activist like Amabel; her rejection of the predominant social values of her age do not make Miriam a revolutionary. In contrast to Amabel's activism, Miriam quietly rejects any orthodoxy, whether social, religious, or political. Amabel, on the other hand, anticipates in a variety of ways the emerging liberated woman of the century; and Miss Richardson's balanced, affectionate, if sometimes lightly ironic, creation of Amabel is adroitly and firmly drawn. Amabel, one of the "new women," is free and ready to join causes which affect females; and she is prepared to suffer (and even to enjoy at times) the consequences. Miriam, in contrast, is too independent to accept another orthodoxy, whether Fabian Socialism or another, because she has struggled to free herself of earlier, albeit more conservative, points of view. Miriam is truly independent in her thinking and, unlike Amabel, refuses to embrace any belief or to stand for any cause which threatens in any way to strip her of her independence. But independence of such purity is not obtained without a price; the cost is loneliness and lack of certainty. She has drawn away from several of her past friendships, and although she judges this to be for the better, it is nevertheless painful. Themes of separation and self-doubt run strongly through *Clear Horizon*. As Miriam reviews her life, she thinks of Amabel, Hypo, and Michael; and she feels that, in retrospect, her relationships with all three were really worthless. Upon finding out that Amabel has been reading her love letters, she is crestfallen as well as indignant; and their friendship appears to be at an end. Densley, who is caring for Miriam's sister Sarah who is quite ill, is struck by Miriam's own poor health which has been brought on by her recent conflicts; he again advises her to go away for a rest. Miriam welcomes the suggestion and prepares to leave London.

As *Pilgrimage* advances, Miriam and Miss Richardson tend more and more to fuse, to become one. Horace Gregory calls this fusion

"Dorothy-Miriam" and refers to the character Miriam as such throughout his study. The distance between author and character becomes almost indistinguishable; and, in spite of the use of third-person narration, character and author are so inextricably related that separation of the two is almost impossible. Appropriately, Miriam's literary interests, sparked originally by Hypo Wilson, become increasingly important. Densley provides a revealing picture of one important aspect of *Pilgrimage* when he suggests that Miriam should begin to write a novel during her stay in the quiet country at Dimple Hill:

"Angles of vision. Yes. You know, you've been extraordinarily lucky. You've had an extraordinarily rich life in that Wimpole Street of yours. You have in your hands material for a novel, a dental novel, a human novel and, as a background, a complete period, a period of unprecedented expansion in all sorts of directions. You've seen the growth of dentistry from a form of crude torture to a highly elaborate and scientific and almost painless process. And in your outer world you've seen an almost ceaseless transformation, from the beginning of the safety bicycle to the arrival of the motor car and the aeroplane. With the coming of flying, that period is ended and another begins. You ought to document your period." (IV, 397)

VI Dimple Hill

Dimple Hill is extremely important because of its revelation of Miriam's intellectual development and her growing confidence in her ability to cope with the cross purposes of life. Miriam, who has left London for an extended vacation, has gone to live on a small farm owned by the Quaker family Roscorla. She has left London in order to "retreat from the superficially dynamic world of external change and new ideas" (IV, 405). In the Quaker tradition, the Roscorla farm is simplicity itself: "The place was not in the least like a farm. A white five-barred gate, fastened back, a sweep encircling a bed of evergreens, grass-bordered, a square plaster house, two-storied, bleak, an enclosed glass porch nakedly protruding, asking, in order that it might blend with the house, a share of the ivy sparsely climbing the left side of the frontage as far as the sill of an upper window" (IV, 433). This initial description of the simple beauty of the farm house characterizes the static serenity of Miriam's entire visit.

During her stay with the Roscorla family, Miriam's life lies suspended as her mind sifts in tranquility the half-conscious memories of her peaceful childhood days, her London friends, and her developing interest in the Quaker religion which startles her in many of its facets. For example, during the Quakers' silent prayer before meals,

She was ready to raise her head. Inexperienced in this form of grace before meat, she raised first her eyes to discover whether the other heads were still bent and found them all, as if with one consent, recovering the upright. As if here, too, as in every human activity there seemed to be, was a concrete spiritual rhythm; so many wing-beats of the out-turned consciousness on its journey towards stillness, a moment's immersion within its pulsating depths, and the return. To a serenity flooding her being and surrounding it, far richer than the same kind of serenity achieved in solitude. It held off the possibility of embarrassment and promised to deal effectually, even though the most tempting opportunity should arise and implore her to seize it, with the desire to make a personal impression. (IV, 469 - 70)

As the days pass with the Roscorlas, Miriam is again and again impressed by their way of life: by "the shock of their loveliness" (IV, 484), by the Quaker religion itself. As she becomes more absorbed in the life at Dimple Hill, her own life has a more meaningful pattern; it becomes not merely a journey through time and space but "a journey that was both pathway and destination" (IV, 485). Her attendance at a Quaker meeting and its experience deepen this feeling and add certainty to her life: "To remain always centered, operating one's life, operating even its wildest enthusiasms from where everything fell into proportion and clear focus" (IV, 497).

In spite of Miriam's admiration for the primitive beauty of the Roscorla farm and her admiration for the Quaker religion and the way of life, she realizes her essential separation from this peaceful way of life. As she sits in the farm's ancient summer house and works at her writing, she thinks of the basic difference between herself and the Roscorlas: "strangers whose ways were not her ways, in whose domain she had pursued, for the whole morning, this alien occupation . . ." (IV, 524). More importantly, Miriam moves ever closer to the profession of her creator; she becomes preoccupied with the idea of a novel, a novel of a special kind; she recalls the words of Bob Greville:

It was Bob, driving so long ago a little nail into her mind when he said, "Write the confessions of a modern woman," meaning a sensational chronicle with an eye, several eyes, upon the interest of sympathetic readers like himself — "Woman, life's heroine, the dear, exasperating creature" — who really likes to see how life looks from the other side, the women's side, who put me on the wrong track and created all those lifeless pages. Following them up, everything would be left out that is always there, preceding and accompanying and surviving the drama of human relationships; the reality from which people move away as soon as they closely approach and expect each other to be all in all. (IV, 525)

Miriam will return, as she must, to London. Amabel and Michael Shatov are married, and Miriam is the happy matchmaker as she watches them create their own small and bright world from the drab elements of London life. Miriam also agrees with Amabel that Ralph Waldo Emerson, despite his independence of thought, is no longer an adequate model for living life in the twentieth century: "Emerson is luminous. Amiable, reasonable, humanistic; incomplete" (IV, 545). *Dimple Hill* recounts an interlude, a peaceful one; but it is clearly only a pleasant stop on Miriam's journey: "even while I pine to stay, I pine, in equal measure, to be gone" (IV, 552). Miriam has learned of the serenity and beauty of the Quaker life; however, her own destiny lies in the activity of her own consciousness — one unsheltered by any metaphysical system.

CHAPTER 6

The Journey Ends

I *Between* Dimple Hill *and* March Moonlight

AFTER the publication of the omnibus edition of *Pilgrimage* in 1938, Miss Richardson was able to devote little time to this work for the remainder of her life; for the war, Alan Odle's health, and other concerns kept her away from the next volume, *March Moonlight*. She did, however, write a number of short stories in her later years. She began writing occasional stories as early as 1919, two of which ("Death" and "Ordeal") were reprinted in the *Best British Short Stories* volumes of 1924 and 1931.[1] It was during the 1940s, however, when she had stopped work on *Pilgrimage*, that Miss Richardson wrote the majority of her shorter works. While her short stories are only a minor part of her literary production and not important in themselves, the later ones reveal in their technique and style the direction *Pilgrimage* was to take between the writing of *Dimple Hill* (1938) and *March Moonlight* (1967). In a story such as "Haven,"[2] which explores the ambiguity and cross-purposes of the simultaneous desire for loneliness and companionship on the part of a writer, Miss Richardson expands her perspective and uses a shifting point of view with an occasional narrator who analyzes the essential disparity between the claims of life and art. "Haven" makes the point that both of these claims must be reconciled, for the character in the story is unable either to live a productive life or to create a work of art because of his failure to come to terms with this dilemma; and, as a result, each becomes an excuse for the failure of the other.

The character in "Haven" is a would-be writer who uses his "projected" work as an excuse to separate himself from all human intercourse. The story is not autobiographical, but the reader can see in it Miss Richardson's attempt to deal with a problem that was not unlike the one which she had resolved in her own life. She had simply given herself up to the nearly full-time care of her husband, Alan Odle, to the detriment of her work. But she did so with pleasure and love, and "Haven" suggests the unhappy, if extreme, alternative.

II   March Moonlight

March Moonlight is an important and interesting work even in its incompleteness; it is not unlike F. Scott Fitzgerald's *The Last Tycoon* in what it reveals of its author's later development and direction. Like *The Last Tycoon*, the author died before being able to finish it; and, although each work reflects substantial development, critical judgment must remain tenuous, since both unfinished works were published posthumously without benefit of their authors' final polishing as well as completion.

In 1938, when the Dent-Cresset omnibus edition was published it was honestly heralded by its publisher as the completed series of highly integrated novels (the word "chapters" was used as well) under the collective title of *Pilgrimage*. In spite of this assurance, however, a number of critics noted that the work seemed inconclusive if not incomplete, in spite of its great length. This vague assertion must have been deeply frustrating to Dorothy Richardson because it confirmed that reviewers, despite many generous comments, really did not grasp or at least accept what she was attempting to achieve in *Pilgrimage*. It should be understood that the charge of "inconclusiveness" was a direct attack on the nature of the work itself rather than merely a stricture against the narrative structure and character development. Reviewers simply had no patience with a work of fiction that continued volume after volume, year after year, with no end in sight. Miss Richardson was, as has been pointed out earlier, convinced of the necessity for an open form in the novel rather than the conclusiveness of the traditional closed form. She believed that the "inconclusiveness" of the work was not only compatible but necessary to the theme — that only in this way could form and content achieve harmony. *Pilgrimage* reflected in its form the inconclusive nature of life itself; and for the work to reach conclusions other than terribly personal ones either thematically or within the fabric of the narrative — was to defeat the most vital element within her work. In 1938, after Proust, Joyce, and Virginia Woolf had become accepted modern masters, the critical charges of inconclusiveness must have been all the more frustrating for Miss Richardson.

The open and seemingly unending and inconclusive form which

Miss Richardson developed with such tenacity raises vital esthetic questions about the relationship between art and life. More to the point, it reflects Dorothy Richardson's own view that esthetic design in its formulation and in its content can and must reflect life's ambiguity, strangeness, cross-purposes — indeed, its very inclusiveness. This concept of esthetic design is not dissimilar to what Yvor Winters, in referring to Joyce, called the "fallacy of expressive, or imitative form," a "fallacy" which Winters believed recurred constantly in modern literature. Miss Richardson's attempt to create this form (which Winters admits is a form, however negative it seems as art) is, of course, subject to the same charge which Winters made against Walt Whitman when he noted that Whitman was trying to express a loose America by writing loose poetry — a procedure which Winters felt led to indiscriminateness at every turn. Nevertheless, Dorothy Richardson, like Joyce, accepted these consequences knowingly and willingly — well aware of the inherent esthetic problems. Such problems appear larger in her work because of her inability to orchestrate the entire organic unity within the fictional world she created, such as giving life to other characters; but she was able through the creation of Miriam Henderson to achieve with real distinction one of the basic elements of fiction — to give breath and life to a character and to make that character live within the world of the novel.

With this background of criticism in mind, one contemplates the long years between the 1938 edition of *Pilgrimage* and the failure of Miss Richardson to publish any additional chapters of *Pilgrimage* during her life time. The publication of *March Moonlight* in 1967 in the reissued omnibus edition does not to any large extent mitigate against the original charges of inconclusiveness, nor does it clarify the esthetic problems which have been discussed above. Horace Gregory, the first critic to analyze *Pilgrimage* in its entirety since the publication of *March Moonlight*, takes a different view from this writer:

"March Moonlight," the last installment of *Pilgrimage*, was not to be published during Dorothy Richardson's lifetime. The manuscript was found among her papers after her death, and though it is impossible to say whether she actually considered it as a final conclusion to her life work, there is good reason to accept it as such. This briefest of the thirteen sections of *Pilgrimage* gathers together all the loose threads left dangling at the end of "Dimple Hill," and seems, indeed, to serve as a coda to the whole work. The span of years in "March Moonlight" is from 1908 to 1915; it covers the events beginning with Dorothy-Miriam's return to London, to her meeting with "Mr. Noble," the man who was to be her husband. Most importantly, it spells out a final confirmation of her attitudes and ideas — a conclusion to her journey, an attainment of maturity.

Her pilgrimage had begun in an aura of guilt — guilt for her mother's suicide, guilt for her sense of shame at her father's humiliation, guilt for her own "differentness." This aura had lingered throughout the course of her early life, throughout the span of years recounted in the first twelve sections of *Pilgrimage*. In "March Moonlight" the guilt is faced, articulated, and, in a sense, overcome.[3]

Gregory's point that *March Moonlight* "gathers all the loose threads left dangling at the end of 'Dimple Hill' " seems far too extravagant a claim for the unfinished work. The work does advance the entire narrative framework of *Pilgrimage*; but, rather than a summary section or a "Coda," it explores new avenues of technique and looks forward to additional developments in the character of Miriam herself. In other words, rather than serving as a conclusion to all of *Pilgrimage*, this "chapter" anticipates developments in Miss Richardson's art and preserves the consistency of the open-form novel which reflects Miriam's continuous journey through life. At the same time, *March Moonlight* retains its continuity and integrity within *Pilgrimage* as a whole; for it explores more complex human dimensions as Miriam matures and develops her interest in writing. Gregory's comment that Miriam sees her life with a new solidity of vision is an important one, but this very notion suggests the growing, expanding awareness of Miss Richardson's creation.

Through the prism of Miriam Henderson's consciousness, *March Moonlight* offers a kaleidoscopic vision of the contrasting worlds of the peaceful Quaker farming family, the Roscorlas, and the London world which Miriam inhabits with her past and present friends. As the past has done throughout *Pilgrimage*, it plays an important role in *March Moonlight*; but Miriam is able in this "chapter" to form a rich synthesis among past, present, and future:

Will begin at once to smite if I pursue the pathway so suddenly opened last night. Towards the past. Inexhaustible wealth. Inexhaustible remorse. Why do they say distance lends enchantment? Distance in time or space does not lend. It reveals. Takes one into heaven, or into hell. From hell, heaven is inaccessible until one has forgiven oneself. So much, much more difficult than accepting forgiveness. Not God, but we ourselves, facing the perspective of reality, judge and condemn. Unforgiven, we scuttle away into illusions. But, all the time, we know. We are perambulating Judgment Days. That will make Jean, the permanent forgiver, laugh till she weeps. But it is the truth. If one could fully forgive oneself, the energy it takes to screen off the memory of the past would be set free.

Perhaps the sudden return of past reality is the result of temporarily losing freedom to move, of being compelled to concentrate, for a whole evening, upon affairs other than my own . . . . (IV, 607)

Equally important, Miriam is able to look outside herself and to make observations without falling into her moods of excessively determined sensibility which marred the earlier sections of *Pilgrimage*. She now sees with a more mature vision and with a writer's awareness the ebb and flow of human existence.

Miriam's determination to be a writer has been a long time in coming, and it is a deeply felt and an acutely understood development, not merely a passing phase. She reveals a clear grasp of the dangers as well as the pleasures of being a writer: "To write is to forsake life. Every time I know this, in advance. Yet whenever something comes that sets the tips of my fingers tingling to record it, I forget the price; eagerly face the strange journey down and down to the centre of being. And the scene of labour, when again I am back in it, alone, has become a sacred place" (IV, 609).

Her sense of interaction between her past and present merges with this deeply felt calling: "While I write, everything vanishes, but what I contemplate. The whole of what I call 'the past' is with me, seen anew, vividly. No, Schiller, the past does not stand 'being still.' It moves, growing with one's growth. Contemplation is adventure into discovery; reality" (IV, 657). Through writing, Miriam has found the ideal vocation to give meaning to her concept of human growth and understanding, for she is able through this art not only to acknowledge the vitality of the past but to shape, mold, and give deeper meaning to life by filtering the past through the present consciousness. This process, of course, has as its concomitants psychological perception and imaginative force; it is the writer who must possess these virtues in abundance, and it is precisely these virtues which Miriam is struggling to possess.

In spite of this "chapter's" fragmentary nature, *March Moonlight* evidences two kinds of growth on the part of its author: first, a certainty of her art which allows her to become more boldly experimental; second, a corollary control over her material which gives dimension and richness to dramatic scenes which she had not achieved previously in *Pilgrimage*. In *March Moonlight*, Miriam's consciousness is allowed to run freely without authorial or third-person intervention. Miss Richardson employs what Richard Ellmann has called Joyce's "blurred margin" technique; that is, the reader is not always certain inside a paragraph whether the sentences are rendered directly by the character or by the author. This technique tends to blur the narrative source, and its effect is to remove, almost completely, authorial intervention and to bring the character's consciousness directly to the surface of the novel. One can conjecture that this delicate technique would have been all the more adroitly and artfully handled had Miss Richardson been allowed to make subtle manuscript changes in a final draft.

The second aspect of development in *March Moonlight* is equally important, especially in view of the author's more open control of character, and of her strong capacity for setting a scene both descriptively and dramatically. For example, the mood of a dinner scene is described with deft penetration which reaches out to a far wider range of significance:

Even at Dimple Hill, she reflected as she roused herself to respond to Sally's remark, bleakness, thrown up from a white tablecoth, hovered above the gathering beneath the summit of the day's light. But only for a moment, only during the settling down of the party separated for the morning and still engrossed, each in his own concerns. After the silence, the dropping of preoccupations and the turning towards the everlasting source within and without, the bleakness was gone. But here, without even the grace whose hurried murmuring by one of the children made, whenever Bennett was present, the unvarying prelude to either of the substantial meals, there was merely the sense of the family gathered together, its natural sympathies and animosities firmly in place, to still the pangs of hunger in a crude light whose dominion could be shattered only by the precarious expedients of human talent; turns, staged to fill the void. (IV, 588)

Miriam is now the conscious observer of people and places; she no longer feels the need to integrate all outside phenomena into the depth of her psyche; and she is able to measure objectively the subtle interplay of human activity.

Perhaps the most revealing evidence of this ability to render a dramatic scene so richly occurs in the meeting between Amabel and

Miriam in Section 3 of *March Moonlight*. In this scene, Miss Richardson is able to convey the emotional import and depth of feeling as well as the subtle tension produced by their meeting; and this feat is accomplished not through extensive dialogue but through Miriam's interior monologue which effectively reveals the dramatic elements of the scene and also conveys the depths of feeling between the two characters. For example,

"Mira."
Something is coming. The low-pitched tone, meditative, revealing her un-
armed and wholly present, means an appeal in the name of the fullest of their past interchange. Some questions that will strike to the centre of one's being. Not in regard to Richard [Roscorlas, at whose farm Miriam is staying]. Considering that episode closed, Amabel would experience, if told how the thought of his share in Rachel Mary's [Richard's sister] invitation reinforced the other inducements to return, the pull of Quakerism, the equal pull of the earth and the light only a contemptuous amazement.
"Will you become a missionary?"
In advance, as ever, of one's own thoughts, she has put the obvious ques-
tion waiting ahead of a full acceptance of Quaker doctrine.
"Your friends will miss you."
Unanswered, she is taking silence for consent, and has moved forward into a future seen by her as in some measure bereft. Believing that I hold, in my consciousness, so much of the drama of her life, an investment that no longer, once I am removed, will yield any return? If now she knew that Jean, unquestioning, trustful of all I may do, stood central in my being, she would rejoice with me? Rejoice that the day of her full power, recalled by the pres-
ent retrospective radiance, is over? (IV, 603 - 4)

Miriam's perceptive mind is thus free to convey totally the scene between herself and Amabel with no authorial intrusion. More significantly, the method is complimentary to the psychological perception revealed within the scene itself; and the technique produces an entire dramatic encounter of emotional and intellectual clarity. Miriam's relationship with Amabel is exceptionally important because Amabel reflects three important facets of her life; her London years of personal freedom and quiet revolt; her involvement with social and intellectual causes and ideas; and her relationship with Michael Shatov and his and Amabel's child who represents a hope for the future. This last facet is an important one, for Amabel's and Michael's baby closes a chapter in Miriam's life:

Yet all such moments, since she [Amabel] knew how thankfully I had given
Michael into her hands, surprise me with their continuous suggestion of
successful rivalry; while still the essence of our relationship remains untouched. Still we remain what we were to each other when first we met.
Something of the inexpressible quality of our relationship revealed itself in
that moment she did not share, the moment of finding the baby Paul lying
asleep in his long robe in the sitting-room, gathered him up, and being
astonished to feel, as soon as he lay folded, still asleep, against my body, the
complete stilling of every one of my competing urgencies. Freedom. Often I
had held babes in my arms; Harriett's, Sally's, and many others. But never
with that sense of perfect serenity. (IV, 658)

For Miriam, the child closes symbolically an important stage of
her life; but, simultaneously, the baby opens a new one since it seals
a bond between her two dearest friends and thus leaves Miriam free
to set upon her life's journey with a feeling of a rich and completed
past which will in turn provide a synthesis with the future.

Thus, *Pilgrimage* ends as it had begun: Miriam is about to set out
again on another journey. The experiences, the torments, the
anguish, and the moments of peace have had their effects on her;
but her long "pilgrimage" is not over — nor will she remain in any
sense a fixed character. The events that have taken place, the people
she has encountered, and her involvements in Germany,
Switzerland, London, and the English countryside have all contributed to Miriam's growth and development. Like Stephen
Dedalus in Joyce's *A Portrait*, she is a moving subject, not a static
figure. Each experience Miriam has facilitates her understanding of
the world and, although seldom immediately, her inner being. In
other words, each detail, or each event, functions to reveal Miriam
not only to the reader but to herself.

Miriam Henderson's "pilgrimage," like Stephen Dedalus' flight,
is, therefore, not over on the last page of the book. Miriam's journey
through life will continue with new trials, new struggles; but inherent in her at the end of *Pilgrimage* is a serenity ("But never with
that sense of perfect serenity"), an understanding of the self. In spite
of a chaotic world and a finite existence, Miriam has found the
courage to be.

CHAPTER 7

Dorothy Richardson's Achievement

W HEN Dorothy Richardson died in 1957, she was hardly remembered by the literary world. The few obituaries that
there were made passing references to *Pilgrimage* and to the fact
that, as an experimental work, it was a forerunner to many of the important novels which were to characterize modern fiction. Unlike
Joyce, Proust, and Virginia Woolf, the great innovators of her
generation, she remained relatively obscure. She lived to be eighty-
four and it had been nineteen years since the omnibus edition of
Pilgrimage was published in 1938. In 1957, she seemed a curious
anachronism rather than a pioneer of the modern novel; and,
although a gradual recognition of Miss Richardson's contribution to
the modern British novel has occurred, her reputation remains even
today a relatively obscure one.

A new perspective on her work has emerged as a result of distance
from it in time and, consequently, the opportunity to see it in the
fuller context of the development of modern British literature. But
John Cowper Powys in his appreciative monograph was able to
isolate as early as 1931 one of Miss Richardson's essential powers and
at the same time to account, at least in part, for her relative
obscurity: "All the way through this extraordinary book the abysmal
difference between the soul of a man and the soul of a woman is
emphasized and enlarged upon. Upon this 'tragic tension,' as
Keyserling well calls it, depends the whole method of Dorothy
Richardson's art. And it is because she has against her the entire
weight of man-made civilization, or, as Spengler would put it, of our
own particular man-made Faustian Culture, that it is so difficult to
win for her, for her daring pioneer-genius, the recognition that we
give so quickly and so easily to conventional charm and conventional
masculine cleverness."[1] Less philosophic reasons can also be
suggested, however, for her lack of recognition; her concentration on

treatment and technique rather than on form; the inescapable boredom because of her insistence on using one character exclusively throughout the great length of *Pilgrimage*; and, finally, the lack of dramatic quality in her fiction imposed by her technique. In rendering almost exclusively the interior world of her character, she was attempting to show that time is not separate from the fluctuations of experience, that the human consciousness creates a simultaneity between present and past, and that the function of art was to illuminate consciousness.

More than most artists, Miss Richardson's work is intricately related to her early experience, and Miriam Henderson's life in *Pilgrimage* parallels Miss Richardson's in almost every detail. Like her creator's, Miriam's life is without great adventure and is often drab; yet, in a very real sense, her life is a "pilgrimage" since Miriam is continually groping for understanding of the self, and is trying to discover what meaning her existence has amid the flux of life in England at the end of the nineteenth and at the beginning of the twentieth century. Each experience shapes in one way or another the character of this mystical young woman, but her encounters with people and her confrontations with ideas are continually seen against social upheaval and intellectual unrest. Miss Richardson shunned dramatic devices in order to concentrate almost exclusively on the inner being of her heroine. This centrality of focus seemed to lack selection and compression at times, but it created the density which she felt was necessary. Her interest in psychology — or, more particularly, the feminine psyche — and her nearly total rendering of a person's inner being in fiction presented insurmountable narrative problems; but, at the same time, Miss Richardson succeeded in accomplishing a great deal of what she had attempted to do, as this study has tried to show. Her precision with language and her adroit rendering of the fluid contours of the human psyche are two outstanding examples of her accomplishment.

Contrary to the then prevailing literary tastes, Miss Richardson was forever repelled by the notion that thoughts and concepts of characters in fiction could easily be expressed in conversation or in simple interior monologue and that such a revelation would establish a novel's significance. She realized that simple opposites could never reconcile the complexity of a character; therefore, if Miriam appears to the reader to be incapable of making a decision, if she is looking to the past as well as to the future, and if she is unable to bring permanent stability to her life, it is important to recognize that these situations are precisely Miss Richardson's purpose. Life is not simple; new decisions are continually fading or melting into newer ones; radical social theories, such as visions of the "new" woman and theological speculation raise more problems for Miriam than they answer. Her "pilgrimage" is for a lifetime; it is a journey with no golden grail as a reward. The meaning of Miriam's life cannot be rendered in platitudes; but it becomes a combination of practical experience, idealism, and a hopeful vision that the individual can find the essential meaning of life as long as she continues to search. This sense of the human predicament is what Miss Richardson tried to express in *Pilgrimage*; and, if this vision of life seems tedious at times, she nevertheless rewards the reader's forebearance with her serious art.

Notes and References

Chapter One

1. Winifred Bryher, *The Heart of Artemis: A Writer's Memoirs* (New York: Harcourt Brace, 1962), p. 168.
2. Ibid., pp. 28 - 29.
3. Gloria Glikin, "Dorothy M. Richardson: The Personal 'Pilgrimage,'" *Publications of the Modern Language Association* 78 (December 1963), 587. I am indebted to Miss Glikin and her biographical studies of Dorothy Richardson; her research and information contributed greatly to the writing of my first chapter.
4. *Pilgrimage* is actually a novel in thirteen volumes or "parts" as Dorothy Richardson referred to them, each with a separate title and self-contained. I have chosen to use the term "chapter" for each title in the interest of clarity. The publishing history is a rather involved one as the parts were published between the years 1915 - 1938. Miss Richardson never stopped writing additional sections which were published in magazines under the title "Work in Progress" and which later became known as *March Moonlight*. The parts and their dates of publication are given in the bibliography. *Dimple Hill* was not published separately, as were the others; it was included in Alfred A. Knopf's four-volume edition of the complete novel that was published in New York in 1938 and in 1967 reissued with a foreword by Walter Allen. The 1967 ed. also contains the previously unpublished — and unfinished — *March Moonlight*. References to *Pilgrimage* indicate only the volume and page number in the four-volume Knopf edition. References to volume and page are placed immediately after the quotation rather than in a footnote.
5. Glikin, p. 588.
6. Ibid.
7. Ibid.
8. Ibid.
9. Ibid.
10. Ibid.
11. "Data for Spanish Publisher," ed. Joseph Prescott, *The Yale Univer-*

sity Library Gazette 33 (January 1959); *The London Magazine* 6, no. 6 (June 1959), 15.

12. Ibid.

13. Glikin, p. 588.

14. Ibid.

15. Richardson, "Data," p. 16.

16. Ibid., p. 15.

17. Ibid., p. 17.

18. Ibid.

19. Ibid., p. 16.

20. Glikin, p. 589.

21. "Data," p. 17.

22. Ibid.

23. Glikin, p. 590.

24. Ibid.

25. Ibid.

26. "Data," pp. 17 - 18.

27. Ibid., p. 18.

28. Glikin, p. 590.

29. "Data," p. 18.

30. Ibid.

31. "Data," p. 18.

32. Unpublished letter from Dorothy M. Richardson to Flora W. Coates (Hillside, Trevone, Padstow, England, 23 April 1948), p. 3. Possession of Thomas F. Staley.

33. "Data," p. 19.

34. Caesar R. Blake, *Dorothy Richardson* (Ann Arbor: University of Michigan Press, 1960), p. 24.

35. Glikin, p. 591.

36. Ibid.

37. Joseph Prescott, "A Preliminary Checklist of the Periodical Publications of Dorothy M. Richardson," *Studies in Honor of John Wilcox*, eds. A. D. Wallace and W. D. Ross (Detroit: Wayne State University Press, 1958).

38. "Data," p. 19.

39. Ibid., p. 18.

40. Glikin, p. 591.

41. P. Beaumont Wadsworth, "A Leader of Modern Realists," *Boston Evening Transcript* (18 August 1923).

42. Glikin, p. 591.

43. Dorothy M. Richardson in an interview by Vincent Brome, "A Last Meeting with Dorothy Richardson," *London Magazine* 6 (June 1959), 28.

44. Ibid.

45. Ibid., p. 29.

46. Dorothy M. Richardson, quoted by Miss Glikin, p. 599.

47. Blake, p. 72.

48. Joseph Prescott, "Seven Letters from Dorothy M. Richardson," *The Yale University Library Gazette* 33 (January 1959), 107.

49. Prescott, "A Preliminary Checklist."

50. Blake, pp. 22 - 23, referring to Rufus M. Jones, *Social Law in the Spiritual World* (New York: George H. Doran Co., 1904), pp. 43 - 79, 97 - 161, 205 - 21.

51. Blake, referring to Rufus M. Jones, "The God of Mystical Experience," in *Pathways to the Reality of God* (New York: Macmillan Co., 1931), pp. 22 - 24.

52. Glikin, p. 592.

53. Ibid.

54. Ibid.

55. Ibid.

56. Ibid., p. 593.

57. Bryher, pp. 236 - 41.

58. Ibid.

59. Ibid.

60. "Data," p. 19.

61. *Pilgrimage*, I, 9.

62. Ibid., p. 10.

63. Glikin, p. 593.

64. Blake, pp. 182 - 83.

65. Unpublished letter from P. Beaumont Wadsworth to Thomas F. Staley (London, England, 30 December 1963), p. 1.

66. Glikin, p. 593.

67. Glikin, quoting from Louise Morgan, "How Writers Work: Dorothy Richardson," *Everyman* (22 October 1931), p. 400.

68. Glikin, p. 594.

69. Ibid.

70. "Data," p. 18.

71. Glikin, p. 594.

72. Ibid., p. 587.

73. Prescott, "Seven Letters," p. 109.

74. Glikin, p. 595.

75. Bryher, pp. 236 - 41.

76. Ibid., p. 168.

77. Unpublished letter from P. Beaumont Wadsworth to Thomas F. Staley (London, England, 30 December 1963), p. 1.

78. Wadsworth, "A Leader of Modern Realists."

79. Unpublished letter from P. Beaumont Wadsworth to Thomas F. Staley (London, England, 22 December 1964), p. 1.

80. Glikin, p. 595.

81. Prescott, "Seven Letters," p. 109.

82. Glikin, p. 596.

83. Unpublished letter from P. Beaumont Wadsworth to Thomas F. Staley (London, England, 22 January 1964), p. 1.

84. Glikin, p. 597.

85. Ibid., p. 596.

86. Ibid.

87. Ibid., p. 597.

88. Ibid.

89. Ibid.

90. Ibid., p. 598.

91. Ibid.

92. Frank Swinnerton, *Figures in the Foreground: Literary Reminiscences, 1917 - 1940* (Garden City, New York: Doubleday and Co., 1964).

93. Glikin, p. 598.

94. Ibid.

95. Ibid.

96. Ibid.

97. Ibid., p. 599.

98. Brome, p. 29.

99. Unpublished letter from P. Beaumont Wadsworth to Thomas F. Staley (Cambridge, England, 1 January 1964), p. 1.

100. Glikin, p. 599.

101. Unpublished letter from P. Beaumont Wadsworth to Thomas F. Staley (Cambridge, England, 20 January 1964), p. 1.

102. Glikin, p. 599.

Chapter Two

1. Alan Friedman, *The Turn of the Novel* (Oxford: Oxford University Press, 1965).

2. Shiv K. Kumar, *Bergson and the Stream of Consciousness Novel* (London and Glasgow: Blackie, 1962), pp. 36 - 37. Although the rhetoric of contemporary philosophy has somewhat clouded Bergson's reputation, his literary influence cannot be discounted.

3. The general confusion on the part of the reviewers may be discerned from reading the following reviews: R. E. Roberts, "Women Novelists," *The Bookman* 59 (February 1921), 202; "Books of the Month," *The London Mercury* 1 (1919 - 1920), 473; "Fiction of Today," *The Saturday Review*, 5 August 1916, p. 138. Most of the reviewers in the teens and twenties were concerned with classifying the amorphous work, a new part of which would come out each year or so.

4. Blake, p. 26.

5. E. K. Brown, *Rhythm in the Novel* (Toronto: University of Toronto Press, 1963), p. 57.

6. Northrop Frye, *Anatomy of Criticism* (Princeton: Princeton University Press, 1957), pp. 187 - 88.

7. Horace Gregory, *Dorothy Richardson: An Adventure in Self-Discovery* (New York: Holt, Rinehart and Winston, 1967), pp. 110 - 11.

8. E. M. Maisel, "Dorothy M. Richardson's Pilgrimage." *Canadian Forum* 14 (June 1939), 92.

9. May Sinclair, *The Little Review,* 4 (April 1918), 3 - 11.

10. Stanley Kunitz, ed. *Authors Today and Yesterday* (New York: W. H. Wilson, 1933), p. 562.

11. Ibid.

12. Robert Humphrey, *Stream of Consciousness in the Modern Novel* (Berkeley and Los Angeles: University of California Press, 1958), p. 78.

13. Ibid.

14. Gregory, p. 111.

15. Ibid., pp. 111 - 12.

16. Ibid., p. 113.

17. James E. Miller, Jr., *The Fictional Technique of F. Scott Fitzgerald* (The Hague: Martinus Nijhoff, 1957), p. 2.

18. H. G. Wells, "The Contemporary Novel," *Fortnightly Review* 96 (November 1911), 862 - 63.

19. For discussion of the problem of time in literature see: Margaret Church, *Time and Reality* (Chapel Hill, North Carolina: The University of North Carolina Press, 1949); William F. Lynch, *Christ and Apollo* (New York: Sheed and Ward, Inc., 1960); Hans Meyerhoff, *Time in Literature* (Berkeley: University of California Press, 1955).

20. Shirley Rose, "Unmoving Center: Consciousness in Dorothy Richardson's *Pilgrimage*," *Contemporary Literature* 10, no. 3 (Summer 1969), 371.

21. Ibid., p. 372.

22. Ibid., p. 375.

23. Joseph Warren Beach, *The Twentieth Century Novel* (New York: Appleton-Century Crofts, Inc., 1932), p. 387.

Chapter Three

1. Of course, there are one hundred cantos in *The Divine Comedy*, but the first canto introduces all three: The Inferno, the Purgatorio, and the Paradiso. Each of the three is made up of thirty-three cantos. For a discussion of the Dante sources, see: Gloria Glikin, "Variations on a Method," *James Joyce Quarterly* 2, no. 1 (Fall 1964), 42 - 49.

2. Henry Pelling, *Modern Britain 1885 - 1955* (London: Sphere Books Ltd., 1969), p. 45.

3. Ibid., p. 44.

4. Maisel, p. 91.

5. Glikin, "Variations on a Method," p. 43.

6. Graham Greene, *The Lost Childhood and Other Essays* (London: Eyre and Spotteswood, 1954), p. 85.

7. T. E. Hulme, "Romanticism and Classicism," *Speculations,* ed.

Herbert Read (London: Kegan Paul, French, Trubner, and Co., Ltd., 1936), p. 120.

Chapter Four

1. Gregory, p. 66

Chapter Five

1. Virginia Woolf, Review of *The Tunnel* by Dorothy M. Richardson, *Times Literary Supplement*, 13 February 1919.

2. Virginia Woolf, *A Writer's Diary* (London: The Hogarth Press, 1953), p. 23.

3. Richard Ellmann and Charles Feidelson, Jr., eds. *The Modern Tradition: Backgrounds of Modern Literature* (New York: Oxford University Press, 1965), p. 123.

4. Woolf, *A Writer's Diary*, p. 46.

5. For excellent discussions of the stream-of-consciousness technique, see: David Daiches, *Virginia Woolf* (Norfolk, Connecticut: New Directions, 1942); Robert Humphrey, *Stream of Consciousness in the Modern Novel*.

6. Ellmann and Feidelson, p. 123.

7. Humphrey, p. 178.

8. Georges Poulet, *The Interior Distance* (Baltimore: Johns Hopkins University Press, 1959), pp. 224 - 25.

9. Gregory, p. 76.

10. Dorothy M. Richardson, *John Austen and the Inseparables* (London: William Jackson Books Ltd., 1930), p. 12.

11. Ibid., p. 16.

12. Ibid., pp. 12 - 13.

13. Ibid., p. 16.

Chapter Six

1. "Death," *Weekly Westminster*, 9 February 1924, p. 466; reprinted in *Best British Short Stories of 1924*, eds. Edward J. O'Brien and John Cournos (Boston: Small, Maynard and Co., 1924), pp. 218 - 20. "Ordeal," *Window: A Quarterly Magazine*, pp. 1 (October 1930), 2 - 9; reprinted in *Best British Short Stories of 1931*, ed. Edward J. O'Brien (New York: Dodd, Mead, 1931), pp. 183 - 89.

2. "Haven," *Life and Letters To-Day* 42 (August 1944), 97 - 105.

3. Gregory, p. 182.

Chapter Seven

1. John C. Powys, *Dorothy M. Richardson* (London: Joiner and Steele, 1931), p. 9.

Selected Bibliography

BIBLIOGRAPHY

A listing of bibliographical sources and materials appears in Joseph Prescott's "A Preliminary Checklist of the Periodical Publications of Dorothy M. Richardson," *Studies in Honor of John Wilcox*, eds. A. D. Wallace and W. O. Ross (Detroit: Wayne State University Press, 1958), pp. 219 - 25. Additional material, both primary and secondary, has been compiled and annotated by Gloria Glickin, *English Literature in Transition* 8, no. 1 (1965), 1 - 35, and *English Literature in Transition* 14, no. 1 (1971), 84 - 88.

PRIMARY SOURCES

1. Autobiography and Letters
"A few facts for you. . . ." In *Sylvia Beach (1887 - 1962)*. [Paris]: Mercure de France, 1963, pp. 127 - 28.
"Beginnings: A Brief Sketch." In *Ten Contemporaries: Notes Toward Their Definitive Bibliography* (second series). Ed. John Gawsworth (pseudonym of Terence Armstrong). London: Joiner & Steele, 1933, pp. 195 - 98.
"Data for Spanish Publisher." Edited by Joseph Prescott. *The London Magazine* 6 (June 1959), 14 - 19.
"Seven Letters from Dorothy M. Richardson." Edited by Joseph Prescott. *The Yale University Library Gazette* 33 (January 1959), 102 - 11.

2. Books
a. Non-fiction
The Quakers Past and Present. London: Constable; New York: Dodge, 1914.
Gleanings From the Works of George Fox. London: Headley, 1914.
John Austen and the Inseparables. London: William Jackson, 1930.

b. Novels
The London publication date appears first; the second date or any dates thereafter refer to United States publication. All American editions, with the exception of *Clear Horizon*, were published under the Knopf imprint.

135

Pointed Roofs. Introduction by J. D. Beresford. London: Duckworth, 1915, 1916. [Introduction by May Sinclair, 1919.]
Backwater. London: Duckworth, 1916, 1917 (New edition 1919).
Honeycomb. London: Duckworth, 1917, 1919.
The Tunnel. London: Duckworth, 1919 [February], 1919.
Interim. London: Duckworth, 1919 [December], 1920.
Deadlock. Foreword by Wilson Follett. London: Duckworth, 1921, 1921.
Revolving Lights. London: Duckworth, 1923, 1923.
The Trap. London: Duckworth, 1925, 1925.
Oberland. London: Duckworth, 1927, 1928.
Dawn's Left Hand. London: Duckworth, 1931.
Clear Horizon. London: J. M. Dent & Cresset Press, 1935. New York: Peter Smith, 1936. In the mid 1930s, Smith published the eleven volumes of *Pilgrimage* which had appeared separately; he purchased sheets from J. M. Dent.
Pilgrimage. London: J. M. Dent & Cresset Press, 1938; 4 vols. 1938. Reissued by Dent and Knopf, 1967. Introduction by Walter Allen. Contains the previously unpublished — and unfinished — thirteenth chapter, *March Moonlight*.

3. Translations
Pointed Roofs. Introduction and notes by Junzaburo Nishiwaki. Tokyo: Kenyusha, [1934].

4. Contributions to Periodicals and Translations
a. Essays
"About Punctuation." *Adelphi* 1 (April 1924), 990 - 96.
"Women and the Future: A trembling of the Veil Before the Eternal Mystery of 'La Giaconda [sic].' " *Vanity Fair* (New York), 22 (April 1924), 39 - 40.
"The Man from Nowhere." *The Little Review* 10 (Autumn 1924 - Winter 1925), 32 - 35.
"What's in a Name?" *Adelphi* 2 (December 1924), 606 - 9.
"Women in the Arts: Some Notes on the Eternally Conflicting Demands of Humanity and Art." *Vanity Fair* (New York), 24 (May 1925), 47, 100.
"Yeats of Bloomsbury." *Life and Letters To-Day* 21 (April 1939), 60 - 66.
"Novels." *Life and Letters To-Day* 56 (March 1948), 188 - 92.

b. Short Stories
"Christmas Eve." *Art and Letters*, 3 (Winter 1920), 32 - 35.
"Haven." *Life and Letters To-Day* 42 (August 1944), 97 - 105.
"Excursion." *English Story: Sixth Series* (1945), 107 - 12.
"Visitor." *Life and Letters To-Day* 66 (September 1945), 167 - 72.
"Visit." *Life and Letters To-Day* 46 (September 1945), 173 - 81.

c. Poems
"Barbara." *Sphere* 95 (13 October 1923), 46. "Three Poems: Sussex —
    Discovery — Barbara." *Poetry: A Magazine of Verse* 27 (November
    1925), 67 - 69.
"Disaster." *Adelphi* 2 (September 1924), 277.

d. Novel (Segments of *March Moonlight*).
"Work in Progress." *Life and Letters To-Day* 49 (April 1946), 20 - 34.
"Work in Progress." *Life and Letters To-Day* 49 (May 1946), 99 - 114.
"Work in Progress." *Life and Letters To-Day* 51 (November 1946), 79 - 88.

e. Translations of Non-Fiction
Man's Best Food by Professor Dr. Gustave Kruger. London: C. W. Daniel,
    1914.
The DuBarry by Karl von Schumacher (Madame Dubarry; Zurich, 1931).
    London: G. G. Harrap, 1932 [February].
Mammon by Robert Neumann. (Die Macht; Leipzig, 1931; Berlin, 1932).
    London: Peter Davies, 1933 [May].
André Gide: His Life and His Works by Leon Pierre-Quint (*André Gide: Sa
    Vie, Son Oeuvre;* Paris, 1932). London: Jonathan Cape; New York:
    Knopf, 1934 [July].
Jews in Germany by Josef Kastein (Pseud. of Julius Katzenstein) Preface
    James Stephens; Translator's foreword, pp. xix - xx. London: Cresset
    Press, 1934 [September].
Silent Hours by Robert de Traz (*Les Heures De Silence;* Paris, 1934). Lon-
    don: G. Bell, 1934 [November].

5. Unpublished Material
Letter to Flora W. Coates from Dorothy Miller Richardson. Written from
    Hillside, Travone, Padstow, England, 23 April 1948. Possession of
    Thomas F. Staley.

SECONDARY SOURCES

Adam International Review 31, nos. 310 - 12 (1966). Issue devoted to
    Dorothy M. Richardson and Proust, also includes a previously un-
    published piece by Dorothy M. Richardson entitled *Old Age.*
AIKEN, CONRAD. "Dorothy Richardson Pieces Out The Stream of Conscious-
    ness of Her Pilgrim, Miriam Henderson." *New York Evening Post* 12
    May 1928, section 3, p. 9. Reported in *A Reviewer's ABC: Collected
    Criticism of Conrad Aiken From 1916 to The Present.* Introduction by
    Rufus A. Blanchard. New York: Meridian, [1958]. pp. 329 - 31.
    Review of *Oberland.* Notes the historic importance of Richardson.
ALLEN, WALTER. *The English Novel.* London: Phoenix, 1954. Points out that
    Richardson was the first of the post-World-War I British novelists who
    deliberately employed the stream-of-consciousness technique.

ALLENTUCK, MARCIA. "Dorothy Richardson on William Blake and the Broadside: An Unrecorded Appraisal." *Blake Studies* 3, no. 2 (Spring 1971), 195 - 96. Allentuck sees Richardson as a "discerning and . . . suggestive critic [of art], especially in her remarks on Blake."

Anonymous. "According to Miriam." *Saturday Review* (London) 24 November 1917, p. 422. See review of *Honeycomb*, p. 11. "Miss Richardson is not without talent but it is the talent of Neurasthenia."

―――. "Fiction. Miss Richardson's New Novel." *Spectator*, 26 March 1921, p. 403. Review of *Deadlock*.

―――. "Fiction of To-day," *Saturday Review* (London), 5 August 1916, p. 138. Review of *Backwater*.

BAKER, ERNEST A. *The History of the English Novel*. 10 vols. New York: Barnes & Noble, 1960 [First published, London: Witherby, 1936], X, p. 356. Places Richardson in the tradition of the psychological novel.

BEACH, JOSEPH WARREN. *The Twentieth Century Novel*. New York: Appleton-Century-Crofts, 1932. Sees the novel largely as imagistic.

BERESFORD, J. D. "Introduction." *Pointed Roofs*, London: Duckworth, 1915, pp. v - viii. A perceptive early, appreciative statement.

BLAKE, CAESAR R. *Dorothy Richardson*. Ann Arbor: University of Michigan Press, 1960. Most thorough study to date; comments on the mystical elements.

BOGAN, LOUISE. "Dorothy Richardson and Miriam Henderson." *New York Times Book Review*, 27 August 1967, pp. 4 - 5. Review of reissued *Pilgrimage* and Gregory's book. Richardson uses "Henry James's viewpoint person," and makes "that person — unchangeably — a woman: herself at one remove."

Anon. "Books of the Month." *The London Mercury* 1 (1919 - 1920), 473.

BOWLING, LAWRENCE EDWARD. "What is the Stream-of-Consciousness Technique?" *Proceedings of the Modern Language Association* 65 (June 1950), 333 - 45.

BROME, VINCENT. *H. G. Wells: A Biography*. London: Longmans, Green, 1951. Discusses the importance of Richardson's relationship with Wells and the accuracy of her portrait of Wells in *Pilgrimage*.

―――. "A Last Meeting with Dorothy Richardson." *London Magazine*, 6 (June 1959), 26 - 32. Brief description of Brome's last meeting with Richardson.

BROWN, E. K. *Rhythm in the Novel*. Toronto: University of Toronto Press, 1963. Excellent background study of the development of image pattern in modern fiction.

BRYHER, WINIFRED. *The Heart of Artemis: A Writer's Memoirs*. New York: Harcourt, Brace & World, 1962. Comments on idea that *Pilgrimage* is the book to read to find out what England was like between 1890 and 1914.

CHURCH, MARGARET. *Time and Reality*. Chapel Hill, North Carolina: The University of North Carolina Press, 1949. Analyzes the conception of time in the modern novel.

DAICHES, DAVID. *The Novel and the Modern World*. Chicago: University of Chicago Press, 1939. Discusses the social background of modern British fiction.

EAGLESON, HARVEY. "Pedestal for Statue: The Novels of Dorothy M. Richardson." *Sewanee Review* 42 (January-March 1934), 42 - 53. First early extended evaluation.

EDEL, LEON. "Dorothy M. Richardson, 1882 - 1957." *Modern Fiction Studies* 4 (Winter 1958), 1965 - 68. Obituary-essay. Literary history "bids fair to use *Pilgrimage* not so much for its exploration of the inner consciousness as for its vivid portraits of certain identifiable figures and its reflection of a certain era in English life and letters."

————. *The Modern Psychological Novel: 1900 - 1950*. New York: Lippincott, 1955. Excellent background study.

————. "Novelists of Influence — VII. Dorothy Richardson Feminine Realist." *Times Educational Supplement* (London), 1 June 1956, p. 743. Essay. Summarizes the decline to critical obscurity of *Pilgrimage* since its beginning forty years before.

FORD, FORD MADOX. *The March of Literature*. London: Allen & Unwin, 1939. Refers to Richardson as an "Abominably unknown contemporary writer."

FREEDMAN, RICHARD. "Dorothy Richardson in Limbo." *Nation*, 25 September 1967, pp. 280 - 81. Review of reissued *Pilgrimage* and of Gregory's book.

FRIEDMAN, MELVIN. "Dorothy Richardson and Virginia Woolf: Stream-of-Consciousness in England." *Stream of Consciousness*. New Haven: Yale University Press, 1955. Good discussion of technique.

FRIERSON, WILLIAM. *The English Novel in Transition*. Norman: University of Oklahoma Press, 1942. In Richardson's fiction the imagist and the stream-of-consciousness technique merge.

GLIKIN, GLORIA. "Dorothy M. Richardson: The Personal Pilgrimage." *Proceedings of the Modern Language Association* 78 (December 1963), 586 - 600. Most important biographical article about Richardson.

————. "Through the Novelist's Looking-Glass." *Kenyon Review*, 31 (Summer 1969), 297 - 319. Richardson is probably H. G. Wells' "most authoritative 'biographer' thus far," even though her portrait of him appears under the guise of fiction in *Pilgrimage*.

————. "Variations on a Method." *James Joyce Quarterly*. 2, no. 1 (Fall 1964), 42 - 49. Essay. Brief comparison of Richardson's *The Tunnel* and *Interim* with Joyce's *Ulysses;* points out the simultaneous serialization of *Interim* and *Ulysses* in *The Little Review* and the resemblances of method in the three novels. Richardson's method probably evolved independently.

GREENE, GRAHAM. *The Lost Childhood and Other Essays*. New York: Viking, 1952. Richardson's method is "ponderous," "undetached," and "unironic"; but there are "passages of admirable description" and "characters do sometimes emerge clearly from the stream-of-consciousness."

GREGORY, HORACE. "An Adventure in Self-Discovery." *Adam International Review* (1966) 31, nos. 310 - 12, 45 - 47. Shortened version of the epilogue of Gregory's book.

———. *Dorothy Richardson An Adventure in Self-Discovery*. New York: Holt, Rinehart and Winston, 1967. Biographical-critical study, for *Pilgrimage* "is closer to the art of autobiography than to fiction." Its personal roots lie deep in her own life, but its "literary roots are decisively English, and are to be found in the writings of Charlotte Bronte."

HUMPHREY, ROBERT. *Stream of Consciousness in the Modern Novel*. Berkeley and Los Angeles: University of California Press, 1954. A basic study on the subject.

HYDE, LAWRENCE. "The Work of Dorothy Richardson." *Adelphi* 2 (November 1924), 508 - 17.

KELLY, ROBERT G. "The Strange Philosophy of Dorothy M. Richardson." *Pacific Spectator* 8 (Winter 1954), 76 - 82.

KUMAR, SHIV K. *Bergson and the Stream of Consciousness Novel*. New York: New York University Press, 1963. In this extended study of Richardson, Kumar finds similarities between her and Bergson but no direct influence.

———. "Dorothy Richardson and the Dilemma of 'Being Versus Becoming.'" *Modern Language Notes* 74 (June 1959), 494 - 501.

MAISEL, E. M. "Dorothy M. Richardson's Pilgrimage." *Canadian Forum* 14 (June 1939), 89 - 92. Brief early study with heavy stress on psychological elements.

MEYERHOFF, HANS. *Time in Literature*. Berkeley: University of California Press, 1955. Affords background as to the way concept of time is dealt with in literature.

MILLER, JAMES E., Jr. *The Fictional Technique of F. Scott Fitzgerald*. The Hague: Martinus Nijhoff, 1957. Especially valuable for its discussion of the Wells-James controversy over "selection versus saturation."

ODLE, ROSE. *Salt of Our Youth*. Cornwall: Wordens of Cornwall, Ltd., 1972. Miss Odle's chapter concerning Dorothy Richardson, éntitled "Alan Odle and Dorothy Richardson," is interesting for its biographical references.

POULET, GEORGES. *The Interior Distance*. Baltimore: Johns Hopkins University Press, 1959. The discussion of time relates well to Dorothy M. Richardson's art.

Powys, John C., *Dorothy M. Richardson*. London: Joiner & Steele, 1931. Compares Richardson's heroine to Faust and to Hamlet in her "female quest for the essence of human experience." She was trying to express fundamental differences between man and woman in their apprehension of life.

Prescott, Joseph. "Dorothy Miller Richardson." In *Encyclopedia Brittanica*, Vol. 19 (1958). Establishes exact dates related to Richardson's life.

Rose, Shirley. "Dorothy Richardson's Focus on Time." *English Literature in Transition* 17 no. 3 (1974), 163 - 72. Miss Rose examines Dorothy Richardson's concept of time as it is expressed in her work, criticism and fiction alike, especially *Pilgrimage*.

————. "Dorothy Richardson's Theory of Literature: The Writer as Pilgrim." *Criticism* 12 (Winter 1970), 20 - 37. The emphasis is upon Richardson's theory about relationship and creative collaboration — between reader and writer and between the writer and himself (as his own reader).

————. "The Unmoving Center: Consciousness in Dorothy Richardson's *Pilgrimage*." *Contemporary Literature* 10 (Summer 1969), 366 - 82. *Pilgrimage* has a "philosophical cohesiveness," the result of Richardson's "imaginative rendering" of the view which persists in all her writing — that the "source and repository of life" is "being," that here lies "immutable reality," apprehended by the "synthesizing capacity of the human consciousness."

Rosenberg, John. *Dorothy Richardson*. London: Duckworth, 1973. A Critical Biography.

Sinclair, May. "The Novels of Dorothy Richardson." *Egoist* 5 (April 1918), 57 - 59. The earliest evaluation of Dorothy Richardson.

Snow, C. P. "Storytellers for the Atomic Age." *New York Times Book Review*, 30 January 1955, pp. 1, 28. Leading article. The "moment-by-moment novel" or "total-recall novel" represents "the most hopeless cul-de-sac in the novel's history," for this form of art "only breathes freely when it has its roots in society." Insists that "sensibility is not enough."

Staley, Thomas F. "A Strange Anachronism." *Adam International Review* 31, nos. 310 - 12 (1966), 48 - 50. Neglect of *Pilgrimage* is unmerited. Each of the parts seems to be a carefully structured work of art in its own right; and the language of the novels "reflects the unclouded rhetoric of an imagist poem."

Swinnerton, Frank. *Figures in the Foreground: Literary Reminiscences, 1917 - 1940*. Garden City, New York: Doubleday and Co., 1964. Good biographical and cultural background.

————. *The Georgian Scene: A Literary Panorama*. New York: Farrar & Rinehart, 1934; *The Georgian Literary Scene: A Panorama*. London: Heinemann, 1935. Assigns to *Pilgrimage* "a place entirely its own" in the "history of modern novels," but asks whether the central character has been "created" or whether she emerges by the "accident of accumulated indications."

TINDALL, WILLIAM YORK. *Forces in Modern British Literature.* New York: Knopf, 1947. Good general background of the social and political forces in Dorothy Richardson's time.

TRICKETT, RACHEL. "The Living Dead — V: Dorothy Richardson." *London Magazine,* 6 (June 1959), 20 - 25. Devises relative anonymity.

WADSWORTH, P. BEAUMONT. "A Leader of Modern Realists." *Boston Evening Transcript,* 18 August 1923. Brief note by someone who knew Dorothy Richardson well.

————. Unpublished letters to Thomas F. Staley. 30 December 1963; 1 January 1964; 20 January 1964; 22 January 1964. This sampling comprises only a part of approximately forty letters from Mr. Wadsworth in my possession.

WOOLF, VIRGINIA. *A Writer's Diary.* Edited by Leonard Woolf. London: Hogarth, 1953. Interesting to compare the work with passages in *Pilgrimage.*

————. Review of *The Tunnel* by Dorothy M. Richardson. *Times Literary Supplement,* 13 February 1919. Virginia Woolf's early assessment.

Index

143